WHY BELIEVE IT?

AN ARGUMENT AGAINST THE TEACHINGS
OF THE IMMORTAL SOUL

JOHN HUFFMAN

WHY BELIEVE IT?
AN ARGUMENT AGAINST THE TEACHINGS OF THE HUMAN SOUL

Bennett books may be ordered through booksellers or by contacting:

Bennett Media and Marketing
1603 Capitol Ave., Suite 310 A233
Cheyenne, WY 82001
www.thebennettmediaandmarketing.com
Phone: 1-307-202-9292

ISBN: 978-1-957114-48-4 (Paperback)
ISBN: 978-1-957114-49-1 (eBook)

Printed in the United States of America

TABLE OF CONTENTS

INTRODUCTION

In this book I analyze the commonly accepted concept of the immortal soul, which I believe detracts from the biblical teaching of the resurrection at the second coming of Christ. Many church denominations today teach this concept without any questions or challenges from the pastorate or laity. It is simply assumed, without anyone looking into the Scriptures to see if this doctrine is supported by the Bible, from which we claim to be getting our doctrines. We need to look into the origin of the concept of the immortal soul, because it does not come from the apostles and their writings. We do, however, have some information about its origin and how the Christian church has picked it up.

This teaching overshadows the doctrine of the resurrection that was proclaimed by the apostles and recorded in their writings in Scripture for us to believe and teach. The immortal soul concept denies the reality of death, which was the consequence of the Fall when Adam sinned as head and source of the human race. God told Adam and Eve that if they ate of the tree of the knowledge of good and evil, they would die that very day (Genesis

1

2:17). Satan questioned that, and told Eve that they would not surely die if they ate it. But death was real, and it came to them as a consequence of their disobedience in eating the forbidden fruit. Romans 5:12 says, "Therefore, just as sin entered the world through one man, and death through sin, and in this way death came to all men," they immediately died spiritually and as mortals began the process of dying that would eventually bring about death physically also. Both of these were the consequences of their sin.

In this book there will be an understanding that the overarching theology is called Incarnational Universal Reconciliation or Restoration. It is about God's grace of desiring to save the whole world. God wills that all be saved and come to the knowledge of the truth (First Timothy 2:4). According to First Peter 1:20, Jesus was chosen before the creation of the world to be our Savior and be revealed in the last days of the Jewish age that ended with the destruction of Judea and the city of Jerusalem in A.D. 70. John 3:16-17 tells us that God so loved the world and sent his only begotten Son with the mission to save the world, not just some out of the world.

Jesus, God's Son incarnate, through his life of obedience, has sanctified our sinful human nature and redeemed mankind from sin and death. In Christ, mankind could be brought back to life spiritually through faith and from physical death at the resurrection. Ultimately God wants mankind restored to the image of God with the human nature unblemished by sin, the nature that God desired for humanity to have in the first place when he created them male and female (Genesis 1:26-27). When Jesus became our Savior, he lived a life of obedience, gave his sinless life through the shedding of his blood for mankind, died and was buried, and then rose triumphantly on the third day to proclaim our redemption from the enemy of death. Because of what he did, he was able to undo the Fall of man and bring life to all men – spiritually in this age, and physically through the resurrection to come when he returns. He was the first resurrected human from the grave of death, and we, as humans, are to follow that pattern in that we are in the process of dying, but when he returns the dead will be resurrected back to life.

The White Throne Judgment is to take place at the Second Coming and resurrection of all mankind. Those who names are written in the book of life will enter the kingdom immediately. Those who have not come to believe in Christ will have to go through a judgment age. This judgment age will run parallel to the kingdom age that Christ establishes when he comes. Those not in the kingdom are those who did not hear the gospel during their lifetime and those who even rejected the gospel or just were not interested in it at the time they heard it. They will be given an opportunity to repent and change their carnal minds to spiritual minds through believing in Christ finally. They will at that time be able to actually see that all that was promised in the gospel announcement has come true for those who believed. First Corinthians 15:24-25 tells us that Christ must reign until he has destroyed all dominion, authority and power. This will be the end of Christ's mission that the Father gave him to bring all to salvation. Christ will then turn the kingdom over the Father and the Son will himself be made subject to the Father that God may be all in all. With this overall picture of God's plan for mankind through the preaching of the gospel, you should be able to see that there is no room for the concept of immortal souls being already judged prior to the White Throne Judgment to an eternity in hell. Christ only judges once and that is at the White Throne Judgment.

Jesus is the pattern for our redemption. When a Christian believes that when he dies he will not really be dead but rather his soul (inner immortal self) will go to heaven to be with Jesus, he is changing the pattern without Scriptural support. What this person believes does not parallel what Christ did to win our victory over death. The immortal soul concept neglects God's solution to man's problem with sin and death.

In this book I will argue the following:

The pagan concept of the immortality of the soul overshadows the biblical teaching of the resurrection, which is that the victory over physical death accomplished by Christ's once-and-for-all sacrifice is to be through the resurrection at his final coming to bring immortality to all mankind.

CHAPTER 1: SURVEY OF THE LITERATURE

A. The concept of the immortal soul

In this overview of literature we want to describe the immortal soul concept. It has overshadowed the doctrine of the resurrection as our hope in Christ, and has brought with it the dualism of soul and body. This immortal soul concept includes the presupposition that death is defined as "the separation of the soul from the body" and that the soul is the non-physical person. Then it is believed that upon the death of the physical body, this non-physical soul departs from the body.

When talking about the Christian, it is believed that the Christian's soul upon death departs to be with Christ in glory. Keddie describes it this way in reference to John 11:25, which reads, "Jesus said to her, 'I am the resurrection and the life. The one who believes in me will live, even though they die.'" He says,

> The death in view here is that of the body. At the moment of death, there will be a continuance of life for the believer. The [Westminster] Shorter Catechism asks, "What benefits do believers receive from Christ at death?" and answers, "The souls of believers

are, at their death, made perfect in holiness, and do immediately pass into glory; and their bodies being still united to Christ, do rest in their graves till the resurrection" (Question 37)[1].

Christians today who believe in the immortal soul assume that there is a location for the departed soul to continue its life existence. The non-physical soul must eventually transition to either heaven or hell (hades), since the soul is believed by them to separate from the body that dies. *The Westminster Confession: A Commentary* states:

The bodies of men after death return to dust, and see corruption; but their souls, (which neither die nor sleep,) having an immortal subsistence, immediately return to God who gave them. The souls of the righteous, being then made perfect in holiness, are received into the highest heavens, where they behold the face of God in light and glory, waiting for the full redemption of their bodies; and the souls of the wicked are cast into hell, where they remain in torments and utter darkness, reserved to the judgment of the great day. Besides these two places for souls separated from their bodies, the Scripture acknowledgeth none.[2]

Holladay says,

At both sophisticated and unsophisticated levels of pagan thought, the body was regarded as the "prison of the soul." Death was considered a welcome relief primarily because it sprang the release of the immortal soul, which would enjoy after-life existence free of the limitations imposed by a physical body. This notion has

---

1 Gordon J. Keddie, *A Study Commentary on John*, Vol. 1 of 2. (Auburn, MA: Evangelical Press, 2001), 427.

2 A.A. Hodge, *The Westminster Confession: A Commentary*, Chapter XXXII, "Of The State Of Men After Death, And Of The Resurrection Of The Dead Section I" (Carlisle, PA: The Banner of Truth Trust, 1869; reprinted 2002), 380.

also penetrated Jewish thought, especially that which was heavily influenced by Greek philosophy (cf. 2 Maccabees 7:9ff.).[3]

It should be pointed out that the only scriptural definition of death is given in James 2:26, which says that the body without the spirit is dead. It is the separation of the spirit that goes back to God that causes death. Those who believe in the immortal soul like to say that the spirit and the soul are interchangeable, but it is quickly objected to by the example of Jesus' death and resurrection. While on the cross, Jesus committed his spirit to the Father in heaven when he was about to die (Luke 23:46), but three days after Jesus' death Mary Magdalene saw the resurrected Jesus and he said for her not to hold him for he had not yet ascended to his Father in heaven. This would mean that the spirit that went back to the Father, who originally gave it, was not Jesus going to heaven at his death. The spirit in man is not the same as the soul which is the person, body and all. The following are verses that indicate that it is the spirit in man, not the soul that goes back to God when a person dies: Ecclesiastes 12:7; Psalms 146:4 and Acts 7:55-59.

B. Belief that the soul separates from the body at death

Early creeds and doctrinal statements of major churches indicate that Christians who believe in an immortal soul also believe in a resurrection at the return of Christ. Between the time of death and that future resurrection, people are in what is generally known as "the intermediate state."

Summers thinks that "disembodied state" is a better term than "intermediate state." What he means by the "disembodied state" is, "the conscious existence of both the righteous and the wicked after death and prior to the resurrection."[4] Summers believes that there is life during what is normally called death. This means that he does not believe that the

---

3   Carl Holladay, *The First Letter of Paul to the Corinthians,* Ed. Everett Ferguson (Austin, TX: Sweet Publishing Company, 1979), 197, 198.

4   Ray , *The Life Beyond* (Nashville, TN: Broadman Press, 1959), 19.

person really dies. The person will always survive the death of the body, even without a body.

This non-physical independent source of consciousness is generally called the immortal soul, though Summers thinks it is best referred to as "spirit," because sometimes the word "soul" means the person himself. He says the two are sometimes interchangeable in the Scriptures.[5]

Summers defines what he means when he speaks of death. He says, "The Greek term θάνατος, translated 'death' means merely 'the separation (whether natural or violent) of the soul from the body by which the life on earth is ended.'"[6] When someone like MacDonald, who believes this view of death, reads a verse such as Philippians 1:23 that says, "I am torn between the two: I desire to depart and be with Christ, which is better by far," he sees this to be saying "that the Christian goes to be with Christ at the time of death and that he is in the conscious enjoyment of the presence of the Lord."[7] This scripture is employed many times in discussion of the immortality of the soul. One who does not believe this (that souls go to heaven when a person dies) will usually say that it means Paul desired to die, knowing that at the resurrection he would be with the Lord. We have Paul's words that tell us when he expects to be with Christ. In Colossians 3:3-4, speaking of believers, which would include him, he says "For you died, and your life is now hidden with Christ in God. When Christ, who is your life, appears, then you also will appear with him in glory."

Lutzer tells us how he thinks Paul spoke of death "as the dismantling of a tent. 'For we know that if the earthly tent we live in is destroyed, we have a building from God, an eternal house in heaven' (Second Corinthians

---

5   Ibid., 6.

6   Ibid.

7   William MacDonald, *Believer's Bible Commentary* (Nashville: Thomas Nelson Publishers, 1995), 1963.

5:1).”[8] He is saying Paul's description refers to our bodies being like a tent that can become tattered and torn, needing replacing. He thinks it is at death that a person departs this tent of a body to a palace in heaven. This is one of the passages that those who believe in the immortal soul use to support their view from Scripture. Yet according to this scripture itself, it tells us that we are longing for a building to replace our destroyed tent, which will not be built with human hands, to cloth us so we will not be found naked. It is speaking of a new spiritual body, which will replace this dying body of flesh that will be given us at the resurrection along with immortality.

Some Christians see some support for this belief of the immortal soul in Luke 16. Spencer shows how the parable of "Lazarus and the Rich Man," which is taken literally by those who hold to the immortal soul, is telling us that Lazarus was still conscious after his death and was in Abraham's bosom. They further see the rich man in hades and being tormented. Normally, hades is equivalent to Sheol in the Old Testament, where it was only referring to the grave. But in this parable, the element of torments can be thought to be a part of the description of a place called hades. Some would understand this parable to be teaching that there is life after death, and that there will be a separation of the blessed from the rebellious or ungodly.[9] They think this is a literal description of the afterlife following what they describe as the separation of the soul from the body at death. We will explain this parable in detail in chapter 10.

C. Belief that eternal punishment awaits the unbeliever

Many people think that unbelievers must be punished for their sins in the afterlife, and reinforced by their understanding of certain biblical passages, therefore they teach that an everlasting, burning hell (Gehenna) is the punishment. Mankind has always tended to believe that evil must

8   Erwin W. Lutzer, *One Minute After You Die* (Chicago: Moody Publishers, 1997), 51.

9   J.A. Spencer, *Five Last Things: Death, Intermediate State (Hades), Resurrection Judgment Eternity,* 3rd ed. (New York: Thomas Whittaker, 1892), 34.

eventually be punished while good should be rewarded. When we come to this subject of the immortality of the soul, we see that this philosophy is applicable. Whether it was pagans of old or Christians today, this duality of a punishment-and-reward system is thought to be necessary.

Dinesh D'Souza offers a presuppositional argument in support of life after death. He says, "humans inhabit two domains: the way things are, and the way things ought to be." He says that humans are moral creatures, unlike animals. He sees natural laws that are controlling our universe, but he recognizes there are moral laws that apply to our behavior. The big difference is the things of the universe are governed by the laws working on them, and this is what science is concerned with. But humans "are internally moved also by 'values.'"[10] Sometimes our behavior goes contrary to what we might think to be natural. Humans may go against their own self-interest because of their acceptance of morality. D'Souza says,

> So how do we explain the existence of moral values that stand athwart our animal nature? The presupposition of cosmic justice, achieved not in this life but in another life beyond the grave, is by far the best and in some respects the only explanation. This presupposition fully explains why humans continue to espouse goodness and justice even when the world is evil and unjust[11]

In the case of immortality of the soul, those who were described as evil or wicked would necessarily go to a place of punishment. The pagans believed hades to be the repository for the dead. Hellenistic Jews in the Roman Empire lived in this culture of pagan religious beliefs and accepted some of the pagan ideas. Eventually these ideas filtered into Jerusalem and

10   Dinesh D'Souza, *Life After Death: The Evidence* (Washington, D.C.: Regnery Publishing, 2009), 166.

11   Ibid., 167.

were picked up by the Pharisees and Essenes.[12] This is how it later became an alternate view of death in the Christian church. Christians who believe this usually think that the dead who have not believed in Christ as their Savior are suffering at this time, and in the final judgment will be cast into the lake of fire.

The description of hades for Christians is said to come from the Bible. Spencer, who believes in the immortal soul, says, "The parable of the Rich Man and Lazarus, moreover, is full of instruction, and gives light on points of deepest interest."[13] He tells us that in this parable we can see that the rich man was in torments while Lazarus was comforted. Therefore, he thinks it can be learned from Luke 16 and Luke 23:43 that hades has two subdivisions, "paradise and the place of misery."[14] A parable is a fictitious story to make a point and is not to be relied on as a literal description of a scene within the story.

We must also note that the paradise mentioned in Luke 23:43 is referring to the time when Christ returns and sets up his kingdom. The thief on the cross did not ask to be with Jesus in heaven but to be remembered when Christ comes into his kingdom at his return. Jesus' reply was, "Truly I tell you today, 'You will be with me in paradise.'" If paradise in heaven was meant then there would be a contradiction in the Scriptures since three days after his death and burial Jesus told Mary Magdalene not to hold to him since he had not yet ascended to the Father in heaven (John 20:17).

Grudem believes that "Although unbelievers pass into a state of eternal punishment immediately upon death, their bodies will not be raised until the day of final judgment. On that day, their bodies will be raised and reunited with their souls, and they will stand before God's throne for final judgment

12 Joseph Agar Beet, *The Immortality of the Soul: A Protest*, 2nd ed. (London: Hodder and Stoughton, 1901), 20-21.

13 Spencer, 34.

14 Ibid., 33.

to be pronounced upon them in the body."[15] He uses the situation of Lazarus and the rich man in the parable of Luke 16 to conclude that no hope is given after one dies and finds themselves in hell (hades). The rich man called out for mercy, but there was no help. Abraham informed him of the great gulf between them, across which the rich man could not come. There was no second chance for the unbelieving dead, according to Grudem, based on this text.[16] Hebrews 6:1-2, listing the elementary teachings of the church, mentions eternal judgment. The literal Greek says, κρίματος αἰωνίου, which literally says age judgment. In English it would be better to use "eon" for age and "eonian" for the adjective form. Therefore, this verse would be saying that we should be believing in an eonian judgment to come. As I will explain later, there will be a chance for unbelievers in this life to have an opportunity after the resurrection of all mankind at the Second Coming of Christ to repent and trust Christ for salvation. Also it is good to note that First Timothy 2:3-6 says, "This is good, and pleases God our Savior, who wants all people to be saved and to come to a knowledge of the truth. For there is one God and one mediator between God and mankind, the man Christ Jesus who gave himself as a ransom for all people."

D. Judgment of unbeliever is justice

Lutzer, a proponent of the immortal soul, reminds us of the judgment of all mankind in Revelation 20:12. He explains that Christ will be the judge and will judge by the light each person had in his lifetime. He doesn't believe that anyone will automatically be saved by their response to general revelation. He believes they must have a personal knowledge of Christ, based on Acts 4:12, which says, "Salvation is found in no one else, for

---

15   Wayne Grudem, *Systematic Theology: An Introduction to Biblical Doctrine* (Grand Rapids, MI: Zondervan, 1994), 824.

16   Ibid., 823.

there is no other name under heaven given to mankind by which we must be saved."[17]

He says that the light given to man by nature is sufficient for judging him, but not for saving him: "Whatever degree of punishment, it will fit the offense exactly, for God is meticulously just. Those who believe in Christ experience mercy; those who do not (either because they have never heard of Him or because they reject what they know of Him) will receive justice. Either way, God is glorified."[18] Lutzer paints a bleak picture for mankind. But this is typical of this view of death.

Lutzer recognizes the seriousness of sin, along with his view of God as being the God of love and mercy. He sees God revealed in the Bible as one who is just, and even those he sends to hell because of their sins will glorify him.[19] He also believes that people in hell (Gehenna) will be in the midst of an unquenchable literal fire and that they will have indestructible bodies so that there will be no relief to their suffering that will last for eternity.[20]

Lutzer explains that hades will be thrown into the lake of fire at the judgment. Those present at judgment will have been resurrected and will have indestructible bodies. He indicates that a literal fire is possible, but there can also be the "fire" of mental anguish of a tortured conscience, or of never satisfying one's desires. On the other hand, "Abraham's bosom" was moved to the presence of Christ at his ascension.[21]

E. Belief that souls of believers go immediately to heaven at death

Sabiers explains the reason why it is thought that when a Christian dies today his soul will depart his body and go to heaven to be with Christ. Remember, some who believe in the immortal soul believe that there are

17   Lutzer, 105, 106.
18   Ibid., 106.
19   Ibid., 109.
20   Ibid., 112.
21   Ibid., 116, 117.

two sections in hades according to Luke 16. Here is Sabiers' explanation: When Christ died, he went to the paradise side of hades. This is reasoned from Luke 23:43, when Christ is said to have promised the thief that he would be with him in paradise along with Acts 2:27, speaking of Christ, says that his soul will not be left in hell (hades). And finally, Ephesians 4:8-10,[22] says:

> This is why it says: "When he ascended on high, he led captive in his train and gave gifts to men." (What does "he ascended" mean except that he also descended to the lower, earthly regions? He who descended is the very one who ascended higher than all the heavens, in order to fill the whole universe.)

He says after this explanation, "We are positive that the righteous dead are no longer in hades, because we know that THEY ARE WITH CHRIST WHERE HE IS."[23]

We can also note that those who have accepted Christ are thought to be rewarded at death. Christians who believe in the immortal soul believe their reward is the crown of righteousness, given upon entrance into heaven to be with Jesus forever. But Second Timothy 4:8 tells us plainly when we will receive the crown of righteousness. It says, " Now there is in store for me the crown of righteousness, which the Lord, the righteous Judge, will award to me on that day—and not only to me, but also to all who have longed for his appearing." So the crown of righteousness is to be received by all believers at the resurrection and Second Coming of Christ, not individually when one dies.

They also use passages in Paul's letters to support this immortal soul view, even when he says in other places that his hope was in the

---

22   Karl G. Sabiers, *Where Are the Dead?: The Bible Answer* (Los Angeles, CA: Robertson Publishing Company, 1940), 40, 41.

23   Ibid., 41, emphasis in the original.

resurrection when Christ appears (Acts 23:6; 24:14-16; 26:6-8). In Acts 23:6 pictures Paul before the Sanhedrin agreeing with the Pharisees that his hope was in the resurrection. Acts 24:14-16 shows Paul before Felix, the governor wherein Paul, referring to the high priest, Ananias, and some elders, who had brought charges against him that he has the same hope in God that they do in that there will be a resurrection of both the righteous and the wicked. Finally, Acts 26:6 showing Paul before King Agrippa, he explains that he is on trial because of his hope in what God has promised their ancestors, namely a resurrection. Paul's hope is seen in these scriptures that his hope was is the coming resurrection at the Second Coming of Christ, not a supposed transition at death to a bodiless continued existence in heaven with Christ. In fact, in Colossians 3:4 he says that that when Christ appears, we who are believers will appear with him. This is when we will be with Christ, not the moment after we die.

Romans 8:23-24 says in Paul's own words,

> We ourselves, who have the firstfruits of the Spirit, groan inwardly as we wait eagerly for our adoption as sons, the redemption of our bodies. For in this hope we were saved. But hope that is seen is no hope at all. Who hopes for what he already has?

Paul's hope was not in an immortal soul that he already had, but his hope was in the resurrection of his life from the dead.

Despite what Paul writes in Romans 8, many Christians think that a person's entrance into heaven takes place upon one's death, since they believe by definition that "death is the separation of the soul from the body." To quote Grudem,

> Death is a temporary cessation of bodily life and a separation of the soul from the body. Once a believer has died, though his or her physical body remains on the earth and is buried, at the moment of

death the soul (or spirit) of that believer goes immediately into the presence of God with rejoicing.[24]

This, of course, is not a definition given in the Bible, but rather is one taken from Plato in his *Phaedo*. In a discussion with Simmias, Socrates replies, "And what is that which is termed death, but this very separation and release of the soul from the body?"[25] This shows that some well-meaning Christians have picked up extra-biblical ideas.

As a result of their mixing biblical ideas and extra-biblical ideas, they have many inconsistencies in what they say. An interesting point is that they believe that those in hades are disembodied souls, and at the resurrection they will be given bodies and then cast into the lake of fire, Gehenna, in which they will suffer torments even more, being in bodies that will not burn up. Grudem tells us that according to Scripture, "There will be a time between our death and the day Christ returns when our spirits [which he says elsewhere are synonymous with "souls"] will temporarily exist apart from our physical bodies."[26] Those who go to hades, according to this, are souls separate from their physical bodies, and will remain so until the resurrection, when the soul is said to be reunited with the body. This is inconsistent with what they think Luke 16 describes hades to be like. The rich man in this parable seems to have a body.

These inconsistencies appear because they are not following Scripture to determine their beliefs. They already have their beliefs and are only picking and choosing scripture passages that are not very clear to assume that they have a rational Scriptural basis for their beliefs. James 2:26 says "As the body without the spirit is dead, so faith without deeds is dead.

24 Grudem., 816.

25 Plato, *The Apology, Phaedo and Crito of Plato*, trans. Benjamin Jowett in *The Harvard Classics*, ed. Charles W. Eliot (New York: P.F. Collier and Son Corporation, 1937), 56.

26 Grudem, 483.

James utilizes the definition of death as the premise to base his doctrinal position that faith without deeds is dead or in vain. There are a number of verses in the Old Testament and the New Testament that show that the spirit in man returns at death to God who gave it. Ecclesiastes 12:7 says, ". . . and the dust returns to the ground it came from, and the spirit returns to God who gave it." Another Old Testament scripture is Psalm 146:4, tells us that when the spirit in man departs that the person's plans are no longer. In the New Testament, we have testimony from Acts 7:55-59 that Stephen prayed that Jesus receive his spirit. Again let me mention that the best example in supporting this is found in Matthew 27:50 when Jesus was about to die, he asked the Father to receive his spirit. We also know that this was not a case of Jesus going to the Father in heaven when he died because in John 20:17 Jesus speaking with Mary Magdalene told her not to hold to him because he had not ascended to his Father in heaven yet.

CHAPTER 2: THE PROBLEM WITH THE TRADITIONAL VIEW

A. It is a denial that one dies

The doctrine of the immortal soul came from pagan sources, not Scripture. It is accepted in many churches and is upheld as an orthodox tradition mentioned in church creeds such as *The Westminster Confession* of the Presbyterian Church. Death is often defined as "the separation of the soul from the body," but this is not found in Scripture. It is part of the philosophy of the Greeks and Plato. With this idea in mind, death becomes a means of deliverance rather than an enemy.

Many Christians today say they will not die; it is just their body that actually dies. This is the same thing that Satan told Eve, that if she ate the fruit of the tree of good and evil she would not die. But God said in the day that you eat of it you will surely die. Spiritually they died that day and began the process of physical death. So believing this way, that one does not really die, only one's body, Christians come to believe that they will be in heaven as a spirit when they die and will only be united with their bodies at the resurrection. Even the Apostles' Creed reads this way. It says that we believe in the resurrection of the body. No, we should believe in the resurrection from the dead like the Nicene Creed says. Christ at the Second Coming will give us a new spiritual body of flesh and bone. This will be a new creation. It will be something that has not been. This is how he gives us immortality. It is from the spirit in man that goes back to God when each of us dies that is to be used at the resurrection to bring about our new bodies that will resemble us but be totally different, durable immortal bodies that will last forever.

This immortal soul concept continues in churches because pastors include the idea in the funeral and memorial services to comfort the bereaved. Church members probably have had this embedded theological understanding most of their lives. Children are taught this from an early age. When a loved one dies, especially a mom or dad, or maybe a grandparent, the child is often told that they are in heaven now. So the child learns that this person didn't really die, but is living somewhere else where we cannot go. If they are brought up in a church that teaches this, it is reinforced. This idea is read into many scriptures to support the immortal soul as being Scripturally based.

B. It offers a false sense of comfort or distress about the dead

At funerals it is believed to be more comforting for the pastor to preach about the deceased loved one being alive in heaven than simply lying in a state of being dead. It comes to leaning towards satisfying one's emotions rather than facing the truth of what the Bible says about death and the resurrection. We are consoled by being told that our loved one is perfectly all right because he is not really dead, but is more alive now than ever before. Death is not defined in the Bible as "the separation of the soul from the body." That came from Plato, not the Bible. Rather than looking to what Plato had to say, we should search the Scriptures regarding death and resurrection.

There is also the negative aspect of the immortal soul for the bereaved who think their loved one was not a believer or church member. They do not recall if he ever confessed his belief in Christ and have not seen any evidence in the deceased's life that would indicate to them that he was a believing Christian. They then have doubts about where he is and what he might be going through.

C. It denies the need for the resurrection

Christ said that he was the resurrection and life (John 14:6), meaning that he alone had the power and would be responsible for bringing us back to life. He was teaching about the resurrection, not about the immortality of the soul. He never mentioned in any of his teachings anything that could be said to be about an immortal soul. Jesus taught that heaven was to come to earth (Matthew 6:20; cf. Revelation 21:1-4), not that we were to go to heaven. There is no mention in Scripture of any soul or person going to heaven when they die.

If we were to ask someone today who is a Christian, what do they think about death. They will probably say that they know where they are going and therefore are not worried about it. I am sure they would also say that they wish to continue living which is natural. But when they say they know where they are going that is an indication that they are thinking about going to heaven, not the grave. They are thinking that they will be fine in heaven with their loved ones who have died earlier. They really have no bad thoughts about dying and going to heaven. Heaven to them is a blessing that happens when we have to die for one reason or another. The point that is made in Scripture is that death is a curse. It is the penalty for sin that started with Adam who was the head of all mankind. Christ will be the second head that will come to bring life to all mankind because of what he has done through his incarnation as a sin free human who did not deserve the death penalty but took it on our behalf to pay the penalty.

Since the penalty has been paid then Christ can release us from death by the resurrection. This is why Matthew 16:18 mentions that the gates of hades will not prevail against the church. This is a metaphorical statement that pictures the triumph of life over death.

D. It weakens the expectation of the second coming of Christ

It would be hard to think that a person who believes he will enter heaven upon his death would have a strong sense of expectation for the return of Christ to resurrect the saints. With the immortal soul, one thinks of going up to heaven individually as a disembodied conscious soul, but the Bible speaks of Christ coming down to raise the dead, everyone at the same time "when he comes" (First Corinthians 15:23) in a general resurrection (John 5:28-29). The emphasis with the immortal soul is on oneself, and one's own inherent qualities, whereas with the doctrine of the resurrection one has to rely on Christ at the second coming to resurrect the dead to imperishable life and to transform the mortal to immortality (First Corinthians 15:52b-53).

E. It teaches everlasting torments for any who have not accepted Christ as Savior

For unbelievers it would mean entering into a place of eternal torment. This causes those who believe in it to make accommodations for it in their witnessing the gospel to others. The gospel, instead of being a message of love and good news, becomes a warning of hell and everlasting torment, and if a person comes to believe that Christ died for his sins, then he will avoid hell when he dies and will be received immediately into heaven and the presence of the Savior. This emphasis on hell is an unfortunate practice of some well-meaning Christians who are taught to witness their faith and understanding to others who may not have accepted Christ as their Savior.

This manner of witnessing to others who do not know the Lord may in fact paint a terrible picture of God. We talk about our loving, gracious

God who loves the sinner and wants him to become an adopted child of his. Yet, from this attempt to witness informs the person witnessed to that God will change his attitude toward one who has not accepted Christ as his savior when he dies. Now God will have him punished in the torments of hell forever because he did not accept God's Son in time. This shows God to be vindictive in getting back at the unconverted sinner by tormenting him forever more.

The gospel is about the hope we have in Christ, who will come back to raise us and all of our loved ones from the dead. Christ has accomplished the victory for us through his life of obedience sanctifying the fallen nature of mankind, through his once-and-for-all sacrifice for our sins, through his resurrection from the dead as the first fruit of all of mankind to be delivered from the bonds of death, and through his ascension to the Father to present us holy and blameless before him. It is good news that Christ has done for us what we could not have done for ourselves.

F. It overlooks God's ultimate plan for the world of mankind

By believing in the immortal soul, people overlook much of the plan of God. God had a plan for humanity on this earth when he created human life, and he knew that it would be corrupted by sin. But God incorporated in his plan that the Son of God would become a human and do for us what we could not do, to bring about our salvation and restore to humanity what was lost at the foundation of the world with Adam and Eve. He wants us to live on earth in complete harmony with each other and with himself. At the resurrection Christ will give immortality to the human race since he has cleansed and sanctified them through his life, death, and resurrection as their Savior, though not all will enter the kingdom at this time. This will wait the culmination of his plan through their eventual belief in Jesus the Christ as their Savior.

Those Christians who believe, and pastors who teach, that we go to heaven when we die overlook that the real plan is for all mankind to one day through Christ live on this earth (Matthew 5:5), not in heaven. Their idea of the goal of man is to believe in Jesus and go to heaven. The resurrection does not hold a prominent place in the general thinking of most Christians today. Their desire is to get to heaven. Heaven is nowhere given in the Bible as our reward or goal in life. N.T. Wright says, "Our citizenship, Paul says, is in heaven, and from there we await the Saviour, the Lord, Jesus the king – which means, despite many misreadings, not that we will in the end go off to heaven, but that the one who is presently in heaven will come back and transform the earth, where we have lived as a colonial outpost of heaven waiting for that day."[27]

Speaking of God's ultimate plan, we should note that it includes the salvation of more than just the church. There are three scriptures that refer to the church as the firstfruits. Second Thessalonians 2:13 says, "But we ought always to thank God for you, brothers and sisters loved by the Lord, because God chose you as firstfruits to be saved through the sanctifying work of the Spirit and through belief in the truth." Here is a second verse in James 1:18: "[18] He chose to give us birth through the word of truth, that we might be a kind of firstfruits of all he created." And here is the third verse that refers to the church of believers as the firstfruits: "Not only so, but we ourselves, who have the firstfruits of the Spirit, groan inwardly as we wait eagerly for our adoption to sonship, the redemption of our bodies." Now let's think about what this means for a moment. For the church to be considered the firstfruits there has to be a larger harvest to follow. That larger harvest must come after the church age if the church is the firstfruit. The larger harvest will be those down through the ages who never heard of Christ, who were born before he ever visited earth. They represent all those

27   N.T. Wright, *Paul: in Fresh Perspective* (Minneapolis, MN: Fortress Press, 2009), 143.

who never believed in Christ even when the gospel was given to them. These are the vast mass of mankind who will still need to be saved through believing on Jesus as their Savior who has accomplished that one-time sacrifice of his death for the sake of the world. John the Baptist said he was the lamb of God to take away the sin of the world. He died on the Passover as our sacrificial lamb that day bearing our sins. Death is the penalty for sin and he bore our sins so that he could later at his Second Coming relieve us of the curse of death by resurrecting all mankind. Then through the judgment age mentioned as something that we should believe as listed in Hebrews 6:2 which in an English translation is eternal judgment. It really should be translated from the Greek as eonian judgment.

The Bible says that Christ is returning to earth with rewards (Hebrews 11:6; Luke 14:14) for those who have been faithful. Scripture tells us that even those who lived prior to the New Covenant have had their sins forgiven, too. Hebrews 9:15 says, "he [Christ] has died as a ransom to set them free from sins committed under the first covenant." With God's plan, through his redemption of all mankind, no matter when they lived, provision has been made for those whom God in Christ through the Spirit has redeemed but they either don't know it or have up to their death rejected the gospel message of salvation for whatever reason. God is a God of love, and it is his will that all men know the truth that Christ died for all mankind (First Timothy 2:3-6) and can freely choose to believe this truth recognizing their inclusion in salvation by grace alone, through faith alone, in Christ alone.

CHAPTER 3: HISTORICAL BACKGROUND OF FIRST CORINTHIANS

We are going to look at portions of First Corinthians 15 to gain a better understanding of what Paul informs us regarding the future resurrection. It is important to begin by understanding the historical and cultural background of the recipients of this epistle before analyzing this chapter. It is also helpful to understand the literary setting of this chapter in which he contrasts the importance of the resurrection to come with Christ's individual resurrection and secondly between the first Adam and the last.

In this chapter, Paul explains the importance of believing in the future resurrection. He starts by reminding the Corinthians that Christ has been raised, which provides the basis for the Christian faith in a future resurrection. If Christ was not raised, we are still in our sins. Paul furthermore explains how death resulting from the first Adam will be overcome by the last Adam, Christ. This passage offers more details about the meaning of the resurrection as the hope of mankind than any other in Scripture. It explains how "in Christ," death will be destroyed and how we will be clothed with immortality.

A. Cultural situation of Corinthian church

There were prostitutes who worked in bars and public bath facilities. It is possible that some of these women were in the congregation as Paul preached about fleeing sexual immorality in First Corinthians 6:12-20. Some of the city also engaged in the slave trade of both male and female prostitutes.[28]

B. Setting of the readers when this was written

After Paul had dealt with the problems about which the church had asked, Paul includes a passage recorded in the fifteenth chapter of Corinthians about the resurrection. He possibly included it because there were some who had denied that there would be a future resurrection (First Corinthians 15:12).[29] This probably stemmed from the body-soul dualism that had become common in Greek society after Plato.

C. Original setting

The occasion for Paul writing this letter was that he had been asked questions from the church. So he was answering their questions. He had heard that there were some problems with regard to the behavior of the members there. He was concerned about division because some were identifying themselves with different individuals as to who they were following. They were carnal minded and exhibited worldly conduct. He needed to deal with these issues before they caused trouble for the church.[30]

28   Pheme Perkins, *First Corinthians, In* Commentaries on the New Testament series (Grand Rapids, MI: Baker Academic, 2012), 9.

29   Leon Morris, *The First Epistle of Paul to the Corinthians: An Introduction and Commentary* in The Tyndale New Testament Commentaries series (Grand Rapids, MI: William B. Eerdmans Publishing Company, 1990), 26.

30   Ibid., 25-26.

CHAPTER 4: LITERARY SETTING OF FIRST CORINTHIANS

A. Genre of First Corinthians

First Corinthians is a letter in its literary form. Letters in the Hellenistic world in which Paul wrote could be business letters, ones addressed as public letters to be read to an audience, and personal letters. Paul is the writer of First Corinthians and he addresses it to the Church in Corinth with the purpose of it being read aloud to them.[31] His purpose in writing it was to answer their questions and to give them valuable instruction to benefit the life of the church. In this letter he dealt with specific situations and he spoke with the authority of an apostle, mentioning this in the first verse of the letter and again in the fifteenth chapter.

B. Literary context

Before First Corinthians 15:12–28, Paul had been explaining the importance of believing in Christ's resurrection and that there was ample evidence that he was raised from the grave on the third day. His resurrection is part of the gospel message he brought to them, and therefore to not accept what he was preaching would be to believe in vain. This leads into the

31   James L. Bailey and Lyle D. Vander Broek, *Literary Forms, in The New Testament: A Handbook* (Louisville, KY: Westminster/John Knox Press, 1992), 23.

passage beginning with verse 12, in which he questions how anyone could not believe in the resurrection of the dead after hearing what he had taught them about Christ being resurrected.

Before beginning the next section of verses 50-58, Paul in verse 49 contrasts the first human, of the dust of the earth, with the second human, whose origin was heaven. This leads into what he is saying beginning in verse 50 about the perishable and the imperishable. Humans descended from the first human are perishable, but through Christ we can be resurrected imperishable from the dead. Gundry says he is talking about perishable physicality. The flesh and blood decompose when one dies. Being raised as imperishable represents the kingdom.[32]

---

32   Robert H. Gundry, *Commentary On The New Testament: Verse-by-Verse Explanations with a Literal Translation* (Peabody, MA: Hendrickson Publishers, 2010), 685.

CHAPTER 5: EXEGESIS OF FIRST CORINTHIANS 15

A. Detailed verse-by-verse analysis of First Corinthians 15:12-28

Verse 12. "But if it is preached that Christ has been raised from the dead, how can some of you say that there is no resurrection of the dead?" This at first may sound like a hypothetical question, but it is not. This is an actual condition that he mentioned in verse 11.[33] He said they preached it and it is believed. So if they believe that Christ was raised from the dead, then they certainly should believe that the dead can be raised. Paul in the previous verses of this chapter has shown specific evidence that Christ was raised from the dead. The resurrection is not impossible, since Christ's resurrection has occurred and there are many still living who will testify to this fact. Even officials who would desire to produce his dead body cannot, and thereby give silent testimony to the fact of his resurrection.

Verse 13. "If there is no resurrection of the dead, then not even Christ has been raised."

---

33 Christian Freidrich Kling, *The First Epistle of Paul to the Corinthians,* trans. Daniel W. Poor. Vol. VI. of *The Commentary of the Holy Scriptures: Critical Doctrinal and Homiletical* series. John Peter Lange, trans. and ed. Philip Schaff. (Grand Rapids, MI: Zondervan Publishing House, 1960), X, 313.

He reasoned from the general premise that if there is to be no resurrection of the dead in the future, then the particular premise of Christ being resurrected cannot be true. If there is no possibility of such a resurrection, then Christ must not have been resurrected.

Verse 14. "And if Christ has not been raised, our preaching is useless and so is your faith." If Christ's resurrection is not true, then our preaching had no meaning and the people's faith in that message was in vain.

Verse 15. "More than that, we are then found to be false witnesses about God, for we have testified about God that he raised Christ from the dead. But he did not raise him if in fact the dead are not raised." If Paul had testified to the resurrection of Christ when he is not actually resurrected, then he and others would be false witnesses about God, since they claimed that it was God who raised Christ from the dead. But if the dead cannot be raised, then God did not raise Jesus from the dead.

Verse 16. "For if the dead are not raised, then Christ has not been raised either." If the dead cannot be raised, then certainly Christ could not have been raised.

Verse 17. "And if Christ has not been raised, your faith is futile; you are still in your sins." We are still in our sins if Christ has not been raised from the dead, regardless of our faith.

Verse 18. "Then those also who have fallen asleep in Christ are lost." Those who have died, even believers, are lost (or another way of translating this Greek word is perished), because they did not receive the benefit of Christ's resurrection for our justification (cf. Romans 4:25). Their death is beyond being restored to life by a resurrection if Christ has not been raised from the dead. Paul uses "fallen asleep" as a metaphor descriptive of death. A dead person looks like one who is sleeping.

Verse 19. "If only for this life we have hope in Christ, we are to be pitied more than all men." If all our hope is limited to just this life, then others should feel sorry for us because there will be no future for us beyond the present life.

Verse 20. "But Christ has indeed been raised from the dead, the firstfruits [the firstfruit in the Greek] of those who have fallen asleep." Now Paul, in contrast to the arguments above, states emphatically that the fact of Christ's resurrection has been thoroughly established by the previous arguments and is significant for the faith and hope of Christians.[34] Christ is the firstfruit, which would imply other fruit to follow in the future. Christ was the first human to rise from the grave of death with an immortal human body. This indicates how we will be resurrected in the future with a similar body.

Verse 21. "For since death came through a man, the resurrection of the dead comes also through a man." Here we have the origin of death, which came through a man, Adam, who sinned, and the origin of the resurrection, which also comes through a man, Jesus Christ. The next verse tells us that all mankind was affected by both Adam and Christ.

Verse 22. "For as in Adam all die, so in Christ all will be made alive."

The same "all" will be brought back to life. The word "all" in the second part of this verse presents an interpretive problem. The question is whether it should be read in the second clause as having the same scope of the one in the first clause. Kling says, "the context does not justify our limiting it to believers in the first clause."[35] The scope of "all" in the first clause pertains to the whole human race in that all are sinners because of Adam and all humans will die without an intervention from God. This is supported by what Paul says in Romans 5:19, "For just as through the disobedience of the one man the many were made sinners, so also through the obedience of the one man the many will be made righteous." Since God has given

34   Ibid., 315.
35   Ibid., 316.

man free will, the degree to which this happens will depend on how man submits to God's call of love and acceptance.

Furnish agrees with what Kling says, and believes that all will be raised at the resurrection. Where some scholars see the phrase "those who belong to Christ" in verse 23 as qualifying that only believers will be raised at this time, Furnish says, "verse 23 reformulates verse 20, where, in his first statement about Christ as the first fruit, Paul refers without any qualification to the resurrection of 'those who have fallen asleep.' Moreover, it directly follows his emphatic declaration that 'all' will be made alive in Christ (v. 22b)."[36] He believes the first statement that "so in Christ all will be made alive" is the main assertion that stands as a guarantee that all the dead will be resurrected. He says, "It is not likely that he means to qualify what he has just said so emphatically and without qualification."[37]

Though some want to limit the "all" of the second clause to refer only to believers, Kling says the phrase "will be made alive" means a resurrection to life in general and would therefore include those resurrected to life and those to judgment.[38] This is consistent with what John says in John 5:28-29.

"In Christ" is often employed as an adjective phrase, specifying believers and their relationship with Christ, but in this verse, "in Christ" is an adverbial phrase denoting that all will be made alive through the agency of Christ, just as death came through the agency of Adam. Being made alive will come solely through the power of Christ.

Christ, as the risen one who is the commencement of the restoration of all human life, constitutes the parallel with Adam. "'Each one' in the next verse, so far as it may stretch even beyond 'those that are Christ's,'

36 Victor Paul Furnish, *The Theology of the First Letter to the Corinthians* (New York: Cambridge University Press, 1999), 111.

37 Ibid.

38 Kling, 317.

seems to require us to take 'all' in the broadest sense, and also to give the broader meaning to 'make alive.'"[39]

Robertson gives us some information about the meaning of 'make alive' in this verse from how it is used in other verses by Paul. He says, "In v. 36 [of 1 Cor. 15], as in Ro. iv. 17, ζωοποιεῖν is used in a natural sense, in John v. 21, vi. 63 in a spiritual sense: in each case the context must decide."[40] John 5:25 and Romans 8:11 could be added to the list of the spiritual uses of this word. Also in Colossians 2:13 and Ephesians 2:5 we have the spiritual sense of being quickened together.[41] Morris says, "*Be made alive* refers to more than resurrection as such. It includes the thought of the abundant life that Christ brings to all who are 'in' him."[42]

Verse 23. "But each in his own turn: Christ, the firstfruits [Grk. firstfruit], then, when he comes, those who belong to him." "But" (δέ) reveals a contrast between "all" in verse 22 and "each" in this verse. It emphasizes that Christ is the first to be resurrected with a new immortal body. It describes him as the firstfruits [firstfruit], which implies he was the first but there will be more to follow in sequence. After his resurrection, "then" there will be a resurrection. It will be when he comes, which is said in other scriptures to occur on the last day. It further specifies the resurrection of those of Christ or who belong to Christ.[43] To "belong" is to be owned by a person or thing. All people belong to Christ since he

39 Ibid.

40 Archibald Robertson and Alfred Plummer, *A Critical And Exegetical Commentary On The First Epistle Of St. Paul To The Corinthians*, in The International Critical Commentary on the Holy Scriptures of the Old and New Testaments series (Edinburgh: T. & T. Clark, 1911) XXXXVI, 353.

41 The Greek word is συνεζωοποίησεν (first person singular form, συζωοποιέω). It means "to make alive together; to make a sharer in the quickening of another, Eph. 2:5; Col. 2:13" (Mounce, 434, 428).

42 Morris, 210.

43 Ronald Trail, *An Exegetical Summary of 1 Corinthians 10-16*, 2nd ed. (Dallas, TX: SIL International, 2001), 292.

redeemed them. Christians were bought with a price (First Corinthians 6:20) and even false prophets were (Second Peter 2:1).

Verse 24. "Then the end will come, when he hands over the kingdom to God the Father after he has destroyed all dominion, authority and power." Does "Then" in this verse imply that there is a time between this resurrection at his coming and the time in which Christ turns over the kingdom to the Father? The question comes up because this Greek word can mean "immediately after" or "at some time after."

(1) Some, such as John MacArthur, say there is an interval of time between the resurrection and the end -- the millennial reign of Christ.[44] This is in accord with the Dispensationalist view of eschatology. In their view this would be a time of Christ putting down his enemies.

(2) Trail points out others say that "the brevity of the phrase εἶτα τὸ τέλος 'then the end' suggests that there is no interval between the resurrection of believers and the end." They would say that the resurrection is a general one of both believers and unbelievers as described in John 5:29 and is therefore one event. Abolishing all authority and dominion and handing the kingdom to the Father are two aspects of the end that occurs at the coming of Christ.[45]

(3) A third view is that "It is impossible to say whether an interval is implied or not since εἶτα 'then' may either indicate something immediately following [or] simply to something just following."[46]

I suggest a fourth view, in which there would be an interval of time between the resurrection and the end, which would be the judgment period (instead of the Millennium suggested by John MacArthur), where Christ would put down all authority, power and dominion. It would be a period

44   Ibid., 293.
45   Ibid., 294-295.
46   Ibid. 294.

where those who are resurrected and yet are spiritually dead could be "made alive" upon acceptance of Christ as Savior and Lord.

Regardless of which view is chosen, it does not affect the thesis of this book: that the hope of humanity is a resurrection, rather than any inherent immortality of souls.

Verse 25. "For he must reign until he has put all his enemies under his feet." Christ at his ascension was given all authority to put down all opposition to God's rule (Matthew 28:18).

Verse 26. "The last enemy to be destroyed is death." Robertson says, "Death is brought to nought when all his victims are restored to life."[47] Symbolically this is expressed in Revelation 20:14 where it is said, "Then death and Hades were thrown into the lake of fire."[48]

Verse 27. "For he 'has put everything under his feet.' Now when it says that 'everything' has been put under him, it is clear that this does not include God himself, who put everything under Christ." "For" ($\gamma\acute{\alpha}\rho$) death was put under Christ's authority, that he could destroy it along with all God's enemies. All things including death were put in subjection to Christ by God. Since it was God who put all things under Christ, God is not included.

Verse 28. "When he has done this, then the Son himself will be made subject to him who put everything under him, so that God may be all in all." At this point the Son incarnate as Christ submits to the Father. He has accomplished his mission as the mediator and redeemer of mankind and in this sense is to be subjected to the Father who sent him. He still remains co-equal with the Father as to his essential being.[49] "That God may

---

47   Robertson, 356.

48   Ibid. Death is to be destroyed, but the annihilation of the wicked would not seem to support that idea. Death would then remain, when this passage is about destroying the concept totally.

49   Trail, 301.

be all in all" is not very clear, but possibly means that God will alone rule everything.[50]

B. Detailed verse-by-verse analysis of first Cor. 15:50-58

Verse 50. "I declare to you, brothers, that flesh and blood cannot inherit the kingdom of God, nor does the perishable inherit the imperishable." "Flesh and blood" is a metaphor referring to the human body and in the context of this passage about the resurrection, would mean that our resurrected bodies need to be different to inherit the kingdom of God. One difference is that our bodies are not going to be subject to decay and death. Paul says in this verse that the term perishable is descriptive of our present bodies, but to inherit the kingdom, they will have to be transformed into imperishable ones.

Verse 51. "Listen, I tell you a mystery: We will not all sleep, but we will all be changed--" A mystery is a truth that has previously been hidden but now is being revealed. In this case God is revealing this mystery through the apostle Paul. He uses the metaphorical term sleep to describe death. Everyone will not die, because one day Christ will return and there will be people alive. Everyone will be changed whether they are dead or alive.

Verse 52. "in a flash, in the twinkling of an eye, at the last trumpet. For the trumpet will sound, the dead will be raised imperishable, and we will be changed." How will this change happen? It will be quick, instantaneous, like a flash, at the last trumpet. This need not be a literal trumpet, but could be a way of indicating Christ's summoning his people, as the trumpet sounded in the Old Testament days.[51] To say the dead will become imperishable also says the contrary of that, which is that the dead are presently perished. Those who alive, and he includes himself (as any of us would do when not knowing whether we would be alive or dead at that time,) will be changed.

---

50   Ibid., 303.
51   Ibid., 340.

Verse 53. "For the perishable must clothe itself with the imperishable, and the mortal with immortality." Paul is describing this change from perishable and mortal, to imperishability and immortality, as if the persons were clothing themselves with this new characteristic.

Verse 54. "When the perishable has been clothed with the imperishable, and the mortal with immortality, then the saying that is written will come true: 'Death has been swallowed up in victory.'" When this change has occurred, then it will be true that "death has been swallowed up in victory," but Paul did not say death has been destroyed. This victory is a reference to what Christ accomplished in his death and resurrection, which eradicated physical death, though the actual fulfillment from our vantage point will only be realized at the resurrection itself. No one will be left dead, and no one will ever die a physical death again, because they have all been made immortal.

Verse 55. "Where, O death, is your victory? Where, O death, is your sting?" Trail says these rhetorical questions are used for the purpose of taunting the personification of death. It is designed as a defiant challenge and mockery to death, which has lost the battle.[52]

Verse 56. "The sting of death is sin, and the power of sin is the law." This reminds us that sin brought about death, and it was by the transgression of the law that labeled an action a sin.[53]

Verse 57. "But thanks be to God! He gives us the victory through our Lord Jesus Christ." We have this hope of victory over death because of our faith in Christ, who has won the victory and will at his coming put an end to physical death.

Verse 58. "Therefore, my dear brothers, stand firm. Let nothing move you. Always give yourselves fully to the work of the Lord, because you know that your labor in the Lord is not in vain." Paul ends this discussion

52   Ibid., 345.

53   Robertson, 378.

of the hope of the resurrection of mankind with an exhortation to stand firm on this teaching and serve our Lord faithfully until then, knowing that whatever we do for him will not be in vain.

CHAPTER 6: HISTORICAL ANALYSIS OF THE IMMORTAL SOUL

A. Extra-biblical idea of immortal soul

The idea of the immortal soul has an ancient history predating the Old Testament of the people of Israel. Beet tells us that the immortality of the human soul was not taught in the Old Testament. He believed, "That man was made in the image of God, by a definite act, and in fulfillment of a deliberate purpose of God, is conspicuously taught in Gen. i:26, 27, ii. 7."[54] He further sees that God created man infinitely superior to animals, but this in no way implies that he has a soul that would continue to exist endlessly.[55]

Genesis 2:7 reads, "Then the lord God formed the man from the dust of the ground and breathed into his nostrils the breath of life and the man became a living being." Man was not given a soul, nor was a soul given a body, but man became a living soul once he was animated with the breath of God. The soul resulted from the entrance of the spirit into the man formed from the soil of the earth. James 2:26 gives us the scriptural definition of death when it says, "As the body without the spirit is dead, so faith without deeds is dead. James based his doctrinal point on this definition of death.

54　Beet, 17.

55　Ibid.

So the conclusion that can be drawn from Genesis 2:7 and James 2:26, is that when the spirit was added to the man formed from soil, he became a living soul and alive, and when this spirit leaves the body, the soul or person becomes dead.

We also know that this soul, or living being, can die or be killed, as shown in Ezekiel 18:4, "For everyone belongs to me, the parent as well as the child—both alike belong to me. The one who sins is the one who will die," and in verse 20, "The one who sins [literally, the soul—the nephesh] is the one who will die. The child will not share the guilt of the parent, nor will the parent share the guilt of the child. The righteousness of the righteous will be credited to them, and the wickedness of the wicked will be charged against them."

The idea of the immortal soul started far back in history. Beet says, "Herodotus, in his bk. ii. 123, recorded that the idea of the immortality of the soul was first taught by Egyptians. They even taught that retribution would occur beyond death for everyone whether good or bad."[56]

D'Souza writes, "In ancient Greece and Rome, the most interesting ideas about the afterlife came not from the temples but from the philosophers. They were based on reason, not revelation. Greek religion had a very weak, diluted concept of the afterlife."[57] Most people are familiar with the writings of Homer, the *Iliad* and the *Odyssey*. Only the gods in these classics were described as immortals. There was a vague notion of life after death in Greek society, but it would be a trip at death "to a shadowy, insubstantial underworld called Hades. In this view, only a fortunate few made it to the Isles of the Blessed, usually heroes who were the offspring of the liaisons of the gods."[58]

---

56 Ibid.
57 D'Souza, 43.
58 Ibid.

B. The development of religions

D'Souza tells us ". . . the fifth century BC, witnessed the spread of Zoroastrianism in Persia, Confucianism and Taoism in China, and Buddhism in India. Hinduism and Judaism also entered a new phase of their development."[59] Judaism at first did not believe in an afterlife. D'Souza, who believes in the immortal soul, thinks it ironic that the Jews, who founded monotheism of the God of life, had to develop the position of a belief in an afterlife. He says the concept of the afterlife developed from their frustration with justice. They didn't see where they were rewarded for their obedience to God's law. They expected to be rewarded in this life with long life and a host of material blessings. God had made promises of a restoration of Israel, and they had expected it to occur on earth in this lifetime.[60] Yet they continued to suffer one devastation or conquest after another. They did not give up on their faith and trust in God, but with the Babylonian Captivity they came to think that rewards and their idea of fairness and justice must come in a postmortem existence on judgment day. They thought some would experience a heavenly reward while others would experience hell (hades).[61]

In the meantime the Greeks had Plato's teachings about the immortal soul. "That the *soul* of man is *immortal* or *deathless,* or in other words that every soul will exist in happiness or misery for endless ages, is a conspicuous feature of the teaching of Plato."[62] But this belief was not universal among the Greeks. Some believed that at death the person would be destroyed and would perish from existence.[63]

---

59   Ibid., 43, 44.
60   Ibid., 44.
61   Ibid., 44, 45.
62   Beet, 1, 2.
63   Ibid.

C. The immortal soul came to Judaism

The immortality of the soul came to Judaism from the Hellenistic influence of the Jews from the Diaspora. They "showed more interest in individual afterlife than in cosmological or nationalistic eschatology."[64]

> JOSEPHUS reports, in his *Wars,* bk ii. 8. II, that the Pharisees believed that the "bodies are indeed corruptible and their substance not abiding, but that the souls continue immortal always;" that the souls of the righteous pass the ocean to a place of rest and blessing, but that the wicked go to a subterranean abode "full of ceaseless punishments." He attributes similar teaching to the Essenes.[65]

Josephus, a Pharisee, wrote a description of pagan hades that the Jews had accepted into their traditions. In this description, we can see the similarity of it with what Jesus described in his parable in Luke 16.[66] This is one of the main scriptures used to pass on this pagan teaching in the name of Christianity. It is a parable and should not be taken literally to be an accurate description of a place of torment for the unrighteous and bliss for the righteous. If taken as a literal description, we have the rich man with a body enduring torments. According to the immortal soul teaching, those in hades should be without bodies until the resurrection and at the judgment are to be cast into *Gehenna,* the lake of fire. Grudem explains that "Death is a temporary cessation of bodily life and a separation of the soul from the body."[67] This is contrary to the picture depicted in Luke 16:24, where the rich man is in torments and asks for a drop of water to cool his tongue. If

64   Everett Ferguson, *Backgrounds of Early Christianity* (Grand Rapids, MI: William B. Eerdmans Publishing Company, 1987), 439.

65   Beet, 20, 21.

66   Flavius Josephus, *Josephus: Complete Works,* trans. William Whiston (Grand Rapids, MI: Kregel Publications, 1960), 636.

67   Grudem, 816.

the rich man is a conscious soul without a body, then his torments would only be mental, not physical. He would not need to have his tongue cooled.

"The Fathers of the church were faced with the unique problem of coming to terms with the very basic Greek notion of the immortality of the soul. The New Testament writers had no such doctrine."[68] Paul, who wrote much of what we call the New Testament, believed in an interim period of time between one's death and the resurrection back to life. He referred to death as a sleep. The resurrection is when the dead would be raised imperishable, or immortal, to live ever afterwards.[69]

Mills says that Oscar Cullmann believed "that the inner man, who has already been transformed by the Spirit (Rom. 6: ff.), and consequently made alive, continues to live with Christ in this transformed state, in the condition of sleep,"[70] which is referring to the afterlife of a believer in the intermediate state before the resurrection. But Mills says this is not what the earliest Christian writers believed. They were reluctant to say much of anything about the sleeping condition of the dead, and they were not interested in the subject of the immortality of the soul.[71]

Ferguson writes,

> The Christian hope for the afterlife is often expressed as the "immortality of the soul" – a phrase that never occurs in the New Testament. Actually the biblical doctrine is of a resurrection of the body. The "immortality of the soul" is more a result of the philosophical (Platonic) tradition and its combination with the idea of resurrection in the church fathers.[72]

---

68 Liston O. Mills, ed. *Perspectives on Death* (New York: Abingdon Press, 1969), 100.
69 Ibid.
70 Ibid.
71 Ibid., 100, 101.
72 Ferguson, 440.

CHAPTER 7: THEOLOGICAL ANALYSIS

A. A theological perspective on the soul

As we get into the theology of the early church, we see that the pagan philosophy of the immortal soul was prevalent in the Gentile communities and, at least in Corinth, was an obstacle to receiving the gospel Paul was preaching. Guthrie says, "Some Corinthians were still maintaining Greek ideas about the immortality of the soul, *i.e.* that after death the soul escaped from the body, to be absorbed into the divine or to continue a shadowy existence in the underworld. To Greeks physical resurrection was impossible (cf. Acts 17:18f., 32)."[73] Acts 17:32 pictures how in Athens, where Plato's immortal soul philosophy was accepted, Paul's mention of the resurrection of the dead was questioned and sneered at.

The New Bible Commentary says that the Christians of the Corinthian area, having endorsed this pagan concept, saw the term "eternal life" mentioned in the gospel as being the same as saying they had an immortal soul. It appeared the gospel was supporting their idea of having an

---

73   D. Guthrie, and J.A. Motyer, eds., *The Eerdmans Bible Commentary,* Consulting eds. A.M. Stibbs and D.J. Wiseman, 3rd ed. (Grand Rapids, MI: Wm. B. Eerdmans Publishing Co., 1970), 1071.

immortal soul. To them, being assured of immortality was the essence of the gospel.[74] This is exactly what many believe today. Actually, the Greek word does not mean eternal life as versions today print, but refers to an age or better in English an eon. "Paul strongly refutes this abberant [sic.] view of the Christian's continuity as an immortal soul apart from one's body by showing that the resurrection of Christ was at the heart of the gospel and the resurrection of the Christian's body was a logical consequence of it."[75]

B. The meaning of soul in the Old Testament

Nepes, or sometimes *nephesh,* is usually translated as "soul" or "life" in the Scriptures. Schultz writes, "*Nepes* in the Old Testament is never the 'immortal soul' but simply the life principle of living being. Such is observable in Gen. 1:20, 21, 24, where the qualified (living) *nepes* refers to animals and is rendered 'living creatures.'"[76]

Nepes is sometimes used in reference to a corpse, as in Numbers 6:6. "More significant here is that *nepes* can mean the corpse of an individual even without the qualification 'dead' (Num. 5:2; 6:11). Here *nepes* is detached from the concept of life and refers to the corpse. Hebrew thought could not conceive of a disembodied *nepes*."[77] When God created man and breathed life into him, man became a living soul (nephesh) or being. He was not a being with a soul.

In Hebrew, a word could be used in different ways with multiple meanings. It was common to use "soul" as a reflexive pronoun, which would be translated by a variety of words such as "I," "me," "self," "one,"

---

74 D.A. Carson, R.T. France, J.A. Motyer, and G.J. Wenham, consulting eds., *New Bible Commentary,* Rev. 4th ed. (Downers Grove, IL: IVP Academic, 2019), 1183.

75 Ibid.

76 Carl Schultz, "Soul," in Walter A. Elwell, ed., *Evangelical Dictionary of Biblical Theology,* (Grand Rapids, MI: Baker Books, 1996), 743.

77 Ibid.

or "being." Many times when we read "soul," it is functioning as a personal pronoun reflecting an individual person.[78]

C. The meaning of soul in the New Testament

Bratcher says, "The Old Testament concept of *nephesh,* which furnishes the basis for the meaning of the New Testament word *psuche,* bears no resemblance to the Greek idea of *psuche* 'soul' as the spiritual part of man, distinct and separate from his material make-up, his fleshly body."[79] The Greek Old Testament use of the word *psuche* refers to an individual, a living person.

The Baker Encyclopedia of the Bible says, "In the NT the word for soul (psyche) has a range of meanings similar to that of the OT. Often it is synonymous with life itself. Followers of Jesus are said to have risked their lives for his (Acts 15:26; cf. John 13:37; Rom 16:4; Phil 2:30)."[80]

The Greek word for soul that is used in the New Testament when it is referring to Old Testament passages is *psyche* (ψυχὴ). Like *nephesh* in the Old Testament, psyche is often translated into English as "life" and as a "person."[81] In Genesis 2:7 it is said that God made man and he became a living soul, meaning a living being. When that verse was translated in the Septuagint, the word *nephesh* was translated as *psyche* (ψυχή). It should be noted that in First Corinthians 15:44, Paul makes a distinction between the σῶμα ψυχικόν, which is the body we now have, and the σῶομα πνευματικόν, which will be the kind of body we will have at the resurrection when Christ returns. The body we now have pertains to the soul, or animal life that

---

78   Ibid.

79   Robert G. Bratcher and Eugene A. Nida, *A Translator's Handbook on the Gospel of Mark* (London: United Bible Societies, 1961), 266.

80   Walter A. Elwell, Gen. ed., *Baker Encyclopedia of the Bible,* anon., "Soul," vol. II. 2 vols. (Grand Rapids, MI: Baker Book House, 1988), 1987.

81   Ibid.

is physical.[82] The body that will be given us at the resurrection will be spiritual,[83] which distinguishes it from the natural body that we have now that is subject to decay and death.

82 William D. Mounce, *The Analytical Lexicon to the Greek New Testament* (Grand Rapids, MI: Zondervan Publishing House, 1993), 487.

83 Ibid., 380.

CHAPTER 8: UNDERSTANDING OF ETERNAL LIFE

A. A Misunderstanding of Eternal Life

Schwartz, who believes in the immortal soul, makes a distinction between the Greek words *psyche* and *zoe*. He says that *psyche*, in the New Testament, is close to *nephesh*, in the Old Testament. To him *psyche* represents the physical life and *zoe* represents the eternal life one receives in Christ.[84] I will critique his view below, but first I will explain what his view is. He shows how he thinks John understood what Jesus was saying by indicating each of these Greek words used in John 12:25 by brackets. John 12:25 reads, "He who loves his life [*psyche*] loses it, and he who hates his life [*psyche*] in this world will keep it for eternal life [*zoe*]."[85] Schwartz suggests that the word *zoe* was used so that "we don't think our present life *(psyche)* will continue forever by its own impetus."[86] He says, "We do not possess eternal life, nor is any part of us eternal. Yet, and this is the great promise and expectation, if we share our life, God will continue giving us

84 Hans Schwartz, *Beyond the Gates of Death: A Biblical Examination of Evidence for Life After Death,* (Minneapolis: Augsburg Publishing House, 1981), 31.

85 Ibid.

86 Ibid., 32.

life *(psyche)* and will preserve our life *(zoe)* into eternity."[87] Though he does not think anyone has an innate immortal soul, he does believe that when one receives Christ he is given the gift of eternal life *(zoe)*. That is, the immortal soul is not inherent within humans, but is given as a gift of grace at the time he receives Christ. If this is true, then how does he account for, according to his theology, unbelievers going to hell as disembodied souls? He said no humans possessed eternal life or immortality unless they have received Christ, and an unbeliever is one who has not received Christ and therefore does not have eternal life nor is immortal according to his concept?

To him eternal life *(zoe)* is not referring to the quality of life one experiences in Christ but it is referring to immortality of the soul without affecting the status of one's mortal body. He believes it is the gift of grace given upon receiving Christ.

B. A Misunderstanding of the Biblical meaning of eternal life

However, E.W. Bullinger in his critical lexicon gives a more traditional view: "Ζωή, [*zoe*] is the life in all its manifestations, from the life of God down to the life of the lower vegetable."[88] He adds, "Each living person or thing has that portion of it which is needful for his or its designed position or purpose. Its one [and] only source is God, who is 'the living One.'"[89] W.E. Vine agrees it "is used in the NT 'of life as a principle, life in the absolute sense, life as God has it, that which the Father has in Himself, and which He gave to the Incarnate Son to have in Himself, John 5:26, and which the Son manifested in the world, first John 1:2'"[90] Vine also explains

---

87 Ibid.

88 E.W. Bullinger, *A Critical Lexicon and Concordance of the English and Greek New Testament* (London: Longmans, Green And Co., 1895), 453.

89 Ibid.

90 W.E. Vine, Merrill F. Unger, and William White, Jr., *Vine's Complete Expository Dictionary of Old and New Testament Words* (Nashville, TN: Thomas Nelson Publishers, 1996), 367.

that due to the fall, mankind has become alienated from this zoe life, but we can through faith in Christ become partakers of it again.[91]

The phrase "eternal life" (*aionios zoe*) literally means "age-lasting life." Vine defines the Greek noun *aion* (αἰών) as "a period of indefinite duration, or time viewed in relation to what takes place in the period."[92] Scripture helps us define the way the words were to be understood at that time. Morrison points out that circumcision (Genesis 17:13), the Sabbath (Exodus 31:16) and the weekly showbread (Leviticus 24:8) observances were all translated to be perpetual or everlasting covenants, but were made obsolete by the establishment of the New Covenant (Hebrews 8:13). He says, "It is unfortunate that translators have used the English words eternal, perpetual, and everlasting, for it is obvious that the Hebrew word *olam* does not mean permanent.[93]

Edward Beecher in his book, *The Scriptural Doctrine of Retribution,* notes that the Septuagint Greek translation of the Hebrew Old Testament was completed three centuries before Christ in Alexandria by 70 translators and was available in Christ's day. He says it equates *aion* with *olam*, the Hebrew word that "is derived from a verb denoting to hide, or to conceal, and denotes a period of time past or future, the boundaries of which are concealed, obscure, unseen, or unknown. So say Taylor and Furst in their Hebrew Concordances."[94] Beecher mentions that it was in the Septuagint that the word *aionios* began to be used extensively:

> And as *aion* denoted an age, great or small, so the adjective *aionios* expressed the idea pertaining to or belonging to the *aion,* whether great or small. Cremer, taking *aion* as denoting

91   Ibid.

92   Vine, 19.

93   Michael Morrison, *Sabbath, Circumcision, and Tithing: Which Old Testament Laws Apply to Christians?* 2nd ed. (Bloomington, IN: iUniverse, Inc.), 98-99.

94   Edward Beecher, *History of Opinions on the Scriptural Doctrine of Retribution* (New York: D. Appleton and Company, 1878), 141-142.

time, defines *aionios* as "belonging to the *aion,* that is, to time in its movement." But in every case this adjective derives its character and duration from the *aion* to which it refers.[95]

The adjective, *aionios,* receives its meaning from the noun form, *aion. Aion* means age, so *aionios zoe* has to mean "age-lasting life" and does not, in itself, necessarily refer to an eternal length of time.[96] Ephesians 2:7 mentions the "coming ages" (the church age and the kingdom age before Christ hands the kingdom to the Father) in the future. A better way to express it in English as a noun and an adjective is by the use of the words "eon" and "eonian" meaning a long undefined period of time. It represents a period of time in which we may not know the beginning or the end of it.

Eternal life, or eonian life, has to do with our spiritual and moral quality of life in Christ. Vine says, "The force attaching to the word is not so much that of the actual length of a period, but that of a period marked by spiritual or moral characteristics."[97] It is best defined in Scripture as in John 17:3, "And this is the life age-during, that they may know Thee, the only true God, and him whom Thou didst send -- Jesus Christ."[98] When we respond to Christ's invitation to follow him, we are given this "life age-during," or eonian life, in the sense that we begin now to live the spiritual life in Christ for this eon with the promise of immortal life at the Second Coming. Immortal life is the kind of life that will be given to us fully in the kingdom eon to come at the resurrection.

The Nicene Creed reflects this same idea. Its last sentence reads: "I acknowledge one Baptism for the remission of sins; and I look for the

95   Ibid., 142.

96   When something takes place within a period of time (the age) there is a beginning and an end, whether we know when it is or not, otherwise we would not see plural phrases such as in Galations 1:5: ᾧ ἡ δόξα εἰς τοὺς αἰῶνας τῶν αἰώνων· ἀμήν (which reads "the ages of the ages.").

97   Vine, 19.

98   Young's Literal Translation.

resurrection of the dead, and the life of the world to come. Amen."[99] We have God's Spirit as our earnest of that life to come. Contrary to what Schwartz was saying, this "eternal life," at least in John's writings, or better translated as eonian life, is not the gift of inherent immortality but the presence of God's Spirit working in our lives since we have accepted the gospel message, and is our earnest of our inheritance and redemption (Ephesians 1:14). Once we respond to Christ in our lives, we are desirous of his Spirit to produce the fruit of the Spirit in our lives (Galatians 5:22-23). We experience the abundant life that God gives us in our new life here with Christ as we live the best we can the kind of life we expect to live in the eon to come.

C. Immortality Coming at the Second Coming

Jesus became the first immortal human, and he is the only one who currently has immortality (First Timothy 6:16). The rest of humanity does not yet have immortality in any form. Jesus, God's Son, came to live the perfect, obedient life, giving his life as atonement for our sins, and being resurrected as the firstfruit of humanity to be resurrected in the future. He plans to give immortality to us at the resurrection (First Corinthians 15:53), which will abolish physical death.

To believe that humans already possess an immortal soul cheapens the salvific work Christ accomplished on our behalf to give us immortality at the resurrection. Christ had to die and be resurrected to save us from being perished forever. Paul says, "And if Christ is not risen, your faith is futile; you are still in your sins! Then also those who have fallen asleep in Christ have perished" (First Corinthians 15:17-18). Our sins would not have been atoned and forgiven, and all humans would have perished as a result of sin without Christ's resurrection.

---

99 Grudem, 1169.

If humans already are immortal souls, which could live on beyond the death of our bodies and go to be in the presence of the Lord immediately at death, why did Jesus have to die and be resurrected for us? Not only did he have to die a physical death for us, but he remained dead for three days. He did not ascend into heaven immediately when he died, but remained in the sleep of death until the third day. He told Mary Magdalene on the morning of his resurrection that he had not ascended to his Father in heaven. Luke, writing the book of Acts, tells us that Peter said that David, the one who had God's heart, had not gone to be with the Lord in heaven. He said that David was dead, buried, and had not ascended to heaven (Acts 2:29, 34a). Like David, the dead are waiting in their graves for the resurrection on the last day. They have not ascended to heaven, nor descended to hell (hades).

CHAPTER 9: ANALYSIS OF SCRIPTURES SAID TO SUPPORT A SEPARATE IMMORTAL SOUL

The following scriptures are a collection of passages that are used to support the immortal soul concept, in that if so, then a Christian would at death merely transition from this physical life to the intermediate state of heaven in another dimension to be in the presence of Jesus. Paul mentions several times in his writings that he would see and be with Jesus when he appeared, not when Paul himself died as to his body but not his soul.

A. Mankind received mortality from Adam

Genesis 2:7 tells us that God made man out of the dust of the ground and breathed into him and he became a "living soul." God breathed life into him. It says the man became a living soul or being, not that he now possessed a soul. The Hebrew word *nephesh* is usually translated as "soul" or "life" in the Old Testament Scriptures. Bratcher says, "The Old Testament concept of *nephesh*, which furnishes the basis for the meaning of the New Testament word *psuche*, bears no resemblance to the Greek idea of psuche 'soul' as the spiritual part of man, distinct and separate from his material make-up, his fleshly body."[100] In other words the biblical use of the word is entirely different from its use in Greek pagan philosophy.

Adam and Eve were given a choice of two trees. They were told not to partake of the tree of the knowledge of good and evil for in the day that they did they would die. When they disobeyed and ate of the fruit of that tree, they immediately died spiritually (sometimes referred to as dying morally). Since they disobeyed becoming sinners themselves, God did not want them to also take of the tree of life and live forever. Had they taken fruit from this tree they would have become immortal. Since God sent them out of the Garden of Eden, they remained mortal and therefore mortality passed upon all mankind, not original sin later taught by Augustine in the 5th century. This means that all of Adam and Eve's descendants would remain mortal and will at some point die physically as a result. Adam physically died when he was 930 years old. The prophet Ezekiel also describes the soul as being mortal. Ezekiel 18:4 says, "The soul that sins, it shall die."

B. The refutation of texts cited to support the immortal soul

1. Since none of us have experienced death, there is a question about existence between death and the resurrection. Are the dead alive in a disembodied condition, or are they really dead? Jesus metaphorically referred to death as a sleep. This is what he said about Lazarus. John 11:14 reads, "So then he told them plainly, 'Lazarus is dead.'" He did not indicate that Lazarus as a soul had departed his body, nor he had gone anywhere. He was just dead, and Jesus resurrected him back to physical life. He was resurrected back to life with the same kind of body, which was subject to mortality, and would eventually die again.

2. There are a number of scriptures that indicate that the dead are unconscious and know nothing of what is going on in our world of the living. Psalms 115:17 reads, "It is not the dead who praise the Lord,

---

100 Bratcher, 266.

those who go down to silence." The psalmist seems to mean that the dead in their graves are silent and unable to worship God. Isaiah 38:18 says, "For the grave cannot praise you, death cannot sing your praise; those who go down to the pit cannot hope for your faithfulness." The psalmist seems to say in this verse that the dead in their graves have lost all abilities to praise, sing, and even hope. There are other verses that could be employed to show unconsciousness, but they are questionable since they lack the context to assure us of what the psalmist means. Context plays a major role in determining the psalmist's meaning, as well as our understanding of the nature of psalms as figurative and poetic.

3. Those, like Sabiers mentioned earlier, who believe in the immortal soul have used Ephesians 4:8: "This is why it says: 'When he ascended on high, he led captives in his train and gave gifts to men,'" to say that at Christ's ascension he led the captives of the paradise section of hades to heaven with him. This would mean that all believers after the time of Christ's ascension would at death go immediately to heaven as an immortal soul to wait the resurrection of their bodies. This verse refers metaphorically of Christ leading all humanity, whether alive or dead physically, who have been the captives of sin and death to the heavenly realms with him, as Paul had said previously in Ephesians 2:6: "God raised us up with Christ and seated us with him in the heavenly realms in Christ Jesus."

However, assuming that Ephesians 4:8 did mean that Christ had emptied paradise and had taken the people there to heaven with him, then that *could mean* that after Christ ascended to heaven, believers would now go immediately as conscious but disembodied souls to heaven when they die. The next point explains why not.

4. From the New Testament we have a passage with context that is clear about what is meant. The apostle Peter says in Acts 2:29, "Brothers, I can tell you confidently that the patriarch David died and was buried, and his tomb is here to this day." And verse 34a reads, "For David did not ascend to heaven." The significance of this passage is that Peter said this after Christ had been resurrected and ascended back to the Father in heaven, and Luke reports it in his Gospel many years later.

5. What about scriptures that do seem to indicate a consciousness in the intermediate state? Isaiah 14:9-10 is one that paints a picture of the grave, or hades, the abode of the dead. This is about the death of the king of Babylon. He was a great powerful person and now he is dead. This is sarcastic in nature and pictures figuratively the dead welcoming him among them. He has been all powerful and was able in his life to subdue and possibly kill them. Now he is their equal in death. It is bitter literary ridicule and was not intended by Isaiah to be taken literally.[101]

6. In the New Testament some point to the sixth chapter of Revelation as an example of the consciousness of saints in heaven. Revelation 6:9-10 reads,

> When he opened the fifth seal, I saw under the altar the souls of those who had been slain because of the word of God and the testimony they had maintained. They called out in a loud voice, "How long, Sovereign Lord, holy and true, until you judge the inhabitants of the earth and avenge our blood?"

This pictures the saints who had been and are being martyred for Christ's sake, and it is assumed by those who believe in the immortal soul concept that they appear to be in heaven as conscious souls, who could speak and cry out, before they are to be united with their bodies in the

101 John Gill, *An Exposition of the Books of the Prophets of the Old Testament,* vol. I. 2 vols. in the *Exposition of the Old Testament,* Vol. V. 6 vols., in the *Exposition of the Old and New Testaments* series, vol. V. 9 vols. 1989; rpt. (Paris, AR: The Baptist Standard Bearer, Inc., 1810), 85, 86

future resurrection. The caution here is to note what kind of literature the book of Revelation is. It is an apocalyptic piece of literature, which means it utilizes a lot of figurative and symbolic descriptions to carry its meaning across to the reader.

These souls, or persons, are said to have and will give their lives for their faith in Christ, and so they are pictured in a religious setting of having spilled their life blood on the altar. The blood of the Old Testament sacrifices was spilled on the altar. "This does not indicate their state or location in the intermediate state. It is just a vivid way of picturing their martyrdom."[102] These souls are figuratively crying out asking for justice from God, just as the blood of Abel cried out to God in Genesis 4:10. These verses are symbolic in nature, and are not to be taken literally as describing the condition of the dead. We should not use symbolic passages to reason that souls are conscious in an afterlife situation.

7.   Philippians 1:21-24 is given as a proof-text showing that Paul believed in the immortal soul. The verse reads:

> For to me, to live is Christ and to die is gain. If I am to go
> on living in the body, this will mean fruitful labor for me. Yet
> what shall I choose? I do not know! I am torn between the two:
> I desire to depart and be with Christ, which is better by far; but
> it is more necessary for you that I remain in the body.

Paul was contemplating death and saw it as a gain for him. But when read in the full context of verses 12 through 24, we can see that Paul's primary desire was not for death, but that Christ is magnified in his life or death. He then realized that he was needed to help these Philippians grow spiritually in the Lord.

These verses can be interpreted that he wanted to depart, or die, and he would immediately be with Christ as a disembodied conscious spirit,

---

102 Ronald L. Trail, *An Exegetical Summary of Revelation 1 – 11*, 2nd ed., vol. XXIII, 24 vols. (Dallas, TX: SIL International, 2008), 158.

but Paul wrote about the crowning event of God's plan for mankind, being the resurrection when Christ returns. He wrote, "just as we have borne the likeness of the earthly man, so shall we bear the likeness of the man from heaven" (First Corinthians 15:49). The resurrection was his hope (Acts 23:6; 24:15; 26:6-8). He knew he would be with Christ only at Christ's appearing when he returns (Colossians 3:2-4). It would be at Christ's return that he would receive a crown of righteousness along with others (Second Timothy 4:6-8), not upon his death.

Paul's meaning is about his being torn between remaining alive and dying, but it does not support the idea of the *soul* departing, which also is not in the context. It was much better for Paul to be safe with Christ in death, knowing that he would be with him in the resurrection, than to be suffering in this age. Paul says in Colossians 3:3, "³ For you died, and your life is now hidden with Christ in God." It is not necessary to read physical proximity nor consciousness into Paul's thought here.

8. Another scripture used to show a conscious soul in heaven is Second Corinthians 12:2-3:

> I know a man in Christ who fourteen years ago was caught up to the third heaven. Whether it was in the body or out of the body I do not know—God knows. And I know that this man— whether in the body or apart from the body I do not know, but God knows—

If he did experience this in the body, then he was actually transported to the third heaven and saw and heard these things he described as inexpressible. He did not rule out the possibility that it was an out of the body experience, either; however, since he did not use the word "soul," he was not speaking of it as if happening after death. It is implied that this event was a vision and revelation from God (v. 1), given while he was in the body, since he mentions that he was at this time given a thorn in the flesh

(v. 7) so he would not be exalted above measure because of the abundance of visions and revelations he had experienced. He says he does not know whether it was a vision, but it was so real to him that he found it hard to say for certain that it was. The verse has no support for any teachings about an immortal soul.

9. Looking at First Thessalonians 5:23 some see Paul saying the person is composed of three elements, "spirit, soul, and body." This passage reads, "May God himself, the God of peace, sanctify you through and through. May your whole spirit, soul and body be kept blameless at the coming of our Lord Jesus Christ." Joel Green explains how Paul is using a parallelism here, not trying to explain the make-up of an individual in three elements:

> The parallelism of the two phrases – "May the God of peace himself sanctify you completely/ /and may your spirit and soul and body be preserved in entirety, free from blame . . ." – signifies that Paul uses these three terms to repeat and expand on the idea of "completely." This is not a list of "parts," then, but a reference to "your whole being."[103]

10. Some speak of going to heaven when they die and receive their crown of righteousness. But this is not what Paul believed would happen, and he says so in Second Timothy 4:8: "Now there is in store for me the crown of righteousness which the Lord, the righteous Judge, will award to me on that day – and not only to me, but also to all who have longed for his appearing." "That day" referred to is the Second Coming of Christ, and he goes on to say that he would not be receiving it alone as would be the case when he would personally die but with "all who have longed for his appearing." This should tell us that we don't die and individually go to heaven to receive our crown of righteousness. In

---

103 Joel B. Green, "Soul," in *The New Interpreter's Dictionary of the Bible,* vol. V. ed. Kathrine Doob Sakenfeld (Nashville, TN: Abingdon Press, 2009), 359.

fact, the writer of Hebrews says in Hebrews 11:39-40 that those heroes of faith in this chapter 11 who had not received what they had been promised, along with those of us who have longed for his appearing, will together receive what was promised and be made perfect. This can only happen at the resurrection and the Second Coming of Christ.

11. John 14:1-23 is another example of a passage that many have thought refers to Christ preparing a place in heaven for Christians to ascend to when they die. Jesus was talking about the idea that there were many dwelling places in his Father's house. Jesus said he was going to prepare a dwelling place for us. But Jesus further said that if he did that, he would come back to us so we could be with him where he would be. This will happen at the Second Coming and resurrection.

But in the meantime, he has prepared a place for us now in this life, which is a relationship with the Father through him. Jesus said that he was in the Father and the Father was in him. The disciples said they did not know how to go where he was going, but Jesus said you do know. The way to the Father where Jesus was going is through him. He was referring to a relationship with the Father through himself. In verse 20 of John 14, he explained what is called the perichoresis relationship with the Father. He said, "On that day you will realize that I am in my Father, and you are in me, and I am in you." This is the relationship that he was talking about setting up between us and the Father. Then in verse 23, he says that we, referring to the Father and himself through the Spirit, will come and make their abode with the believer. We have that relationship with the Father now through Jesus who lives in us through the Holy Spirit.

12. We want to explain Second Corinthians 5:1-10, which is another passage used to say a believer's soul at death departs its body and goes to heaven. The subject is Paul's desire to exchange his old earthly body for a new heavenly body at the resurrection so he could live with the Lord.

His desire was to have this earthly body changed at the resurrection to a heavenly or spiritual body, and then he would be with Christ bodily forever. He did not desire a bodiless (unclothed) life while his body was in the grave. He is talking about the resurrection to a new life with an immortal body, where he can live by sight in the presence of the Lord in the kingdom of God. He had said in First Corinthians 15:53-54,

> For the perishable must clothe itself with the imperishable, and the mortal with immortality. When the perishable has been clothed with the imperishable, and the mortal with immortality, then the saying that is written will come true: "Death has been swallowed up in victory."

This is the clothing that he was speaking of in this passage. When Paul later said in verse 8 that he "would prefer to be away from the body and at home with the Lord," he was using an euphemism for death as a preference as opposed to what he was experiencing in this life in his frail human body. He would prefer the time in the future when he would have a new resurrection body that would be incorruptible. This is explained later in our comments to Second Corinthians 5:1-5, 8 in this chapter that it will be from heaven.

Just because he mentioned "and at home with the Lord" does not mean that this event would occur at the same time as his death. Other scriptures he wrote indicate his desire for the day of resurrection and his presence at that time with the Lord at the Second Coming (First Thessalonians 4:16-18). Mentioning Colossians 3:4 again from Paul's writings, it tells us when he thought believers would appear in glory. It would be at the resurrection and appearing of Christ, not before.

13. Hebrews 9:27-28 says: "And just as each person is destined to die once and after that comes the judgment [of the White Throne]." There is no mention of an intermediary judgment to get into heaven or hell.

Christ was sacrificed to take away the sins of the world. Romans 5:18-19 says: "Consequently, just as one trespass resulted in condemnation for all people, so also one righteous act resulted in justification and life for all people. For just as through the disobedience of the one man the many were made sinners, so also through the obedience of the one man the many will be made righteous." Verse 19 says the "many" were made sinners and that the same "many" will be made righteous." We know that all mankind was made sinners because of Adam's sin, so therefore, all mankind will be made righteous. So says, 1 Corinthians 15:22. "For as in Adam all die [or "are dying" in the Greek], so in Christ all will be made alive." This passage is verified by the Greek word for word.

Christ will appear a second time without sin to those waiting for him for salvation. This is when we receive salvation from death which is the penalty of sin (Romans 6:23). Christ did not die in our place, or we would not have to die. He died for our sake and left the death penalty in place even though he has already paid it. It will be removed at the Second Coming when Christ then raises the dead to immortality.

14 Revelation 20:15 tells us, at the Second Coming and resurrection, death and hades (the grave) will be thrown into the lake of fire. Death and the grave are abstract nouns and cannot be destroyed in a literal fire. This is a figurative fire indicating the total destruction of these two abstract nouns. There will never again be any physical death with bodies needing a grave. All are made immortal at Christ's appearance. Those unbelievers whose names are not written in the book of life will be judged and casted into this figurative lake of fire to hopefully bring about their conversion since they will actually see and know Christ where we had only faith that Christ died for us and will come back for us.

15. Acts 2:27 is a quote from David saying: "My body also will live in hope because you [God the Father] will not abandon me to the grave nor will you let your Holy One see decay. So he is saying that God the Father will not leave his soul (his person, himself) in the grave. And the soul, Jesus as an individual or person, died and was buried in a grave. Revelation 16:3 says, ". . . every living soul died in the sea wher the second angel poured out his bowl on the sea. The living soul, or person or individual, can die as Jesus did. The word "soul" is used as a pronoun standing for the person who is an individual. *Myself* is an example of a reflexive pronoun when written as my soul. Again, Ezekiel 18:4 says, "For every living soul belongs to me, the father as well as the son – both alike belong to me. The soul [a pronoun standing for the person or individual] who sins is the one who will die."

16. Luke 23:46 shows us that the spirit in man is not interchangeable with the soul. The Bible says many times that at death the spirit in man goes back to the Father who gave it but never says that the soul goes back to the Father who gave it. When Jesus gave up his spirit, it went back to the Father in heaven who gave it. But John 20:17 tells us that this was not an example of Jesus going to heaven because he told Mary Magdalene not to cling or hold him at this time because he had nct yet gone to his Father in heaven and this was three days after his death. This also contradicts what we are told Christ said to the thief on the cross. So Christ did not meet with this thief that day in heaven and the thief did not ask to be with Christ in heaven that day. He asked Jesus to remember him when he, Jesus, would come *into* (the Greek word is εἰς) his kingdom at the Second Coming. Verses referring to Jesus coming in judgment always use the word "in," (εν in Greek). Therefore, since punctuation is determined by the translator, the comma should be moved and the phrase should be written like this: "I tell you the truth today, you shall be with me in paradise." The kingdom to be established on this earth at the return of Christ will be a paradise.

17. **John 17:24** refers to these who are given to him as the church, his bride. They will be where he should be as a man at the Second Coming and resurrection. They will be in the Kingdom of God/Heaven on this earth. So hereafter the saints in their own persons, and with their own eyes, shall see him as he is, and appear in the glory of heaven on earth with him.

18. **Revelation 7:13-17** is another prophecy given to John who wrote it down and sent it to the Asia Minor Christian churches to warn them of things to come. This scripture does not say they died in the Great Tribulation but rather that they are coming out (a present participle in the Greek) of the Great Tribulation having been washed in the blood of Christ depicted by having washed their robes and made them white in the blood of the Lamb.

19. It is correct to say, as **John 5:24** says, that he who ". . . believes him who sent me has eternal [eonian] life and will not be condemned; he has crossed over from death to life." He has crossed over from spiritual death to spiritual life. His name will be in the book of life and he will not be judged, but will be received into the Kingdom of Heaven on this earth at the White Throne Judgment. The phrase "eternal life" is misleading. This says when we receive Christ or believe in Christ we have αἰώνιον [eonian] life. This word expresses an indefinite period of time. It is the Christ-life for the age, the church age. Once Christ returns the believer will receive immortal life in order to enter the Kingdom, which means he does not have immortality now.

20. In **2 Corinthians 5:1-5,** Paul is expressing his desire to exchange this earthly body one day for a spiritual body of flesh and bone reserved in heaven. He says that he at no time wants to be unclothed, or without a body. He says that while we are in this tent or body, we groan for to be clothed with our heavenly dwelling from (ἐξ means "from") heaven. First Corinthians 15:44 says that we are sown a natural or soul body (σῶμα ψυχικόν, body soul) but raised a spiritual body. The body that was buried will not be resurrected. The dead will be resurrected and given a body from heaven.

21. In **Ecclesiastes 12:1-7,** looking first at verse 7 which says, ". . . and the dust returns to the ground it came from, and the spirit returns to God who gave it." The soul was the person and now the body of the person is in the grave and the person no longer exist as a living person. The English word eternal in this verse is the Hebrew word *olam*. Olam is usually translated in English Bibles as forever, perpetual and everlasting or eternal. The word actually could only mean an indefinite period of time, or as long as certain conditions last, according to Scriptural contexts. For example, the Old Covenant Law of Moses was made obsolete (Hebrews 8:13) by the New Covenant. Circumcision was commanded to last forever using this word. The festivals and sacrifices were commanded also to last forever using this word that really refers to an indefinite period of time. Then man goes to his olam [indefinite] home, the grave. It is indefinite because he will be there indefinitely until the resurrection but it will not be permanent. The people in the Old Testament thought of dying and going to "sheol," the grave.

22. **First John 3:2** says that when he appears at the Second Coming he will make us immortal like his body was after his resurrection, a spiritual body of flesh and bone.

23. **Matthew 22:31-32** starts out by saying, "And as for the resurrection of the dead. . . ." That is in respect to, or in reference to, the resurrection, ". . . I am the God of the living." Abraham, Isaac and Jacob are dead now, but at the resurrection they will again be alive because of the power of God (v. 29), which is what he said the Sadducees' error was because they were known not to believe in the resurrection since it is not mentioned in the Torah

24. Matthew 17:1-8 is about the Transfiguration of Moses and Elijah and Jesus. Peter, James and John probably recognized Moses and Elijah from what they had heard in stories in Scripture and from their dress or something like that which indicated who they were and their role in the past because they had not personally ever seen or met them. These individuals though had not been raised from the dead. Verse 9 reads, "Then as they were coming down the mountain, Jesus instructed them, 'Tell no one the vision [ὄραμα], until the Son of Man is risen out from the dead.'"

25. In looking at **First Peter 3:18-22**, we need to ask some questions to hone in on what this passage is actually saying. For instance, does this passage actually tell us that Jesus preached to those in prison? Secondly, does it tell us where this preaching took place? And thirdly, who were these spirits in prison?

First, this verse clearly says that Jesus was made alive, or resurrected, by the Holy Spirit. It does not say that he was still alive while his body reclined in death. Some will say that Jesus was under the power of death and yet at the same time was actively alive preaching to dead spirits in hades. He was not under the power of death if actively alive in hades carrying on all the activities that he could do while he was alive above ground. No, Jesus did not do the preaching. The soul of Jesus, the individual that he was when alive, was dead all over and lying in a tomb until he was made alive (resurrected) by the (Holy) Spirit on the third day.

Secondly, it says, *through which.* The Greek word for *which* is neuter in Greek to match *Spirit* as the antecedent which is neuter also and not *Jesus* which is masculine. Since we are now talking about the Holy

Spirit, *he* in our translation should be translated as *it,* which is neuter to also refer to the Holy Spirit who preached to the spirits in prison in the days of Noah while the ark was being prepared. Genesis 6:3 says that the Spirit spent 120 years trying to reach the people of that time. Then Genesis 6:7 says, "So the Lord said, 'I will wipe mankind, whom I have created, from the face of the earth – men and animals, and creatures that move along the ground, and birds of the air – for I am grieved that I have made them.'"

Thirdly, we need to determine to whom did the Spirit preach? In Luke 4:18-19, Jesus declared that he came to proclaim liberty to the captives (prisoners of sin). Isaiah 14:17 makes reference to the King of Babylon who overthrew cities and ". . . would not let his captives go home?" Captives of sin are prisoners too. These prisoners that were preached to by the Spirit in the days of Noah were mortals according to Genesis 6:3, and that the Spirit contended with them for 120 years before destroying mankind with the exception of Noah and his family.

So now this whole passage should make perfect sense in that it was not the dead Jesus, but the Spirit, that preached, not to the dead at that time, but to fallen mankind in the days of Noah.

26. Verse 3 in **First Peter 4:3-7** begins talking about our life being controlled by the flesh having passed. That life now passed, was one of following the will of the nations (pagan, worldly practices), having been in lack of self-control, lusts, drunkenness, reveling in drunken sprees and unlawful idolatries.

Verse 4 says that kind of life being passed for you, they who still live that way are surprised that you are not running together into the same wastefulness, excess and blaspheming ways. Notice that these people referred to are living.

Verse 5 says that it is these who will give an account to the one in readiness to judge the spiritually living and the spiritually dead. The word "now" appears in some translations but it is not found in the Greek text. It is an example of an interpretation given by the translator.

Verse 6 says that for this purpose also was the gospel preached to them, the living who were spiritually dead, that they might be judged indeed according to men in the flesh, but they might live according to God in the Spirit. So the purpose of preaching the gospel to them is to bring about a change in their life. They would have the opportunity through hearing the gospel to repent and believe the gospel and change their lives from following the flesh to following the ministry of the Spirit.

Peter now warns us in verse 7 that of all things the end has drawn near. You should be sound-minded therefore, and be sober in your prayers. Peter was probably warning of the tribulation coming in A.D. 67 – 70 ending with the destruction of Judea and Jerusalem along with the temple.

C. CONCLUSION

None of these passages offer support for an immortal soul when understood within their immediate context and within the overall context of what Paul says elsewhere in the New Testament regarding when he expects to be with Christ and receive his reward.

Many today have tried to turn the enemy of death into their hope of being transported to heaven when they or their loved ones die, but Paul's hope was not to die and immediately be taken to heaven. In Acts 23:6-9, when he was before the Sanhedrin, he sided with Pharisees, saying that his hope was in the resurrection of the dead.

In Acts 24:14-16, Paul standing before Felix, again sided with the Pharisees, saying that he had the same hope in God as these men did in that there will be a resurrection of both the righteous and the wicked, a general resurrection of all mankind at once that is also mentioned in John 5:28-29.

Finally, in Acts 26:6-8, Paul before King Agrippa this time, said that he had the same hope as the Jews who were accusing him. He asked: "Why should any of you consider it incredible that God raises the dead?"

There is no notion of an immortal soul taught in the Old and New Testament Scriptures, and these passages from Paul plainly tell us that his hope was in the resurrection to come at the Second Coming of Christ. Furthermore, this is when Paul believed he would receive the crown of righteousness and immortality. How can we believe otherwise?

CHAPTER 10: THE PARABLE OF LAZARUS AND THE RICH MAN

This is another scripture employed to give support to the idea of the continuing life after death of the body and needs to be explained. Luke 16:19-31 is a parable of Jesus about the Pharisees and how they always felt their importance and superiority. They were men of position and power in the Jewish community. They didn't take time to think about the poor and the less fortunate like the beggar who sat at the gate asking for alms.

Jesus had warned the Pharisees before that they would one day see Abraham, Isaac and Jacob in the kingdom and themselves being cast out and there would be weeping and gnashing of teeth (Luke 13:27-28). Weeping would indicate one's sorrow and gnashing of teeth would be an emotional reaction of disgust with oneself for having missed the kingdom because of his stubbornness in rejecting Christ, not from being in the torments of hell, which is usually taught by this parable.

A. A PARABLE ABOUT RESURRECTION

Here Jesus is portraying this in a parable of the future resurrection to life and to judgment (the general resurrection mentioned in John 5:28-29) in that this rich man, depicting the Pharisees, is resurrected to judgment, rather than into the kingdom. This judgment will be for the purpose of repentance and reconciliation by lovingly chastising him and cleansing him of his sinful nature. First Timothy 2:3-4 says that it is . . . God our Savior, who wants all people to be saved and to come to a knowledge of the truth.

Jesus says, "in the grave [the hades in which Jesus was buried, Acts 2:26-27] he lifts up his eyes." In other words, in the grave he awakes in the resurrection to judgment and he sees Abraham and Lazarus a far off in the kingdom while he is being thrust out just like what Jesus had said about them earlier. His torment is not from being literally in a fire but perhaps the one like Paul described in First Corinthians 3:13-15 that would try his works on that day, which would cause mental torment or suffering (odunomai) where his tongue swells, his mouth becomes dry and he is in a cold sweat fearing what is about to take place. These are all symptoms of mental anguish, not physical torture. If he were in the hell like most people think the Bible relates, he wouldn't be just weeping and gnashing his teeth, but would be screaming with excruciating pain such that he would be unable to engage in this calm discussion with Lazarus.

B. NO ONE HAS INHERITED THE PROMISED LAND

The term *bosom* (usually defined as an embrace) symbolizes Lazarus' intimate relationship with Abraham. As Christian believers we are said to have this same intimate relationship now because Abraham and his descendants were promised an inheritance of land on this earth. We too are heirs waiting for the fulfillment of that promise. Stephen said in his speech in Acts 7:2-5 that God called Abraham to the land of promise where he sojourned with Isaac and Jacob who were also named as heirs, but they all died without receiving the promised inheritance (Hebrews 11:8-13). Abraham was then and still is to this day dead (John 8:52) and has not inherited the promised land. He will not until Christ returns and resurrects him and all mankind at that time. Hebrews 11:39-40, referring to a list of

Old Testament people who endured many things but remained faithful to death, says:

> [39] These were all commended for their faith, yet none of them received what had been promised, [40] since God had planned something better for us so that only together with us would they be made perfect.

C. CONCLUSION

This parable is to be a warning, not only to the Pharisees but to all who refuse to accept Jesus for who he is. The rich man even asked Abraham to send Lazarus to his brothers to warn them of this resurrection to judgment, but was told that they have Moses and the prophets (the Old Testament Scriptures) and if they do not listen to that they will not be convinced if someone was raised from the dead. Jesus had said that the Scriptures foretold of him. They showed without a doubt that Jesus was the fulfilment of the prophetic description of the Messiah, yet these Pharisees were rejecting him.

This was a lesson to the Pharisees whom he pictured in this parable as the rich man. Jesus described them as not caring for others, but only about themselves, but most importantly he made the point that they were still rejecting him as the Son of Man when they should have known better from the Scriptures and the miracles he had performed. In fact, sometime earlier, Jesus raised a man from the dead whose name was also Lazarus (John 11:39-44) and a friend of Jesus. Ironically, it was because of this miracle that the Pharisees began plotting to kill Jesus (John 11:45-55), and even Lazarus as well (John 12:10-11).

JOHN HUFFMAN

CHAPTER 11: NO ONE HAS ASCENDED TO HEAVEN

When we read and study the Scriptures, we do not expect to find verses or passages that contradict one another. We believe the Scriptures were inspired by the Holy Spirit. We certainly do not expect any scriptures to contradict what Jesus said plainly. Yet, many today accept universally that Enoch and Elijah were translated into heaven even though Jesus said as recorded in John 3:13 "And no one has ascended into heaven but the Son of Man who came down from heaven." If we do not accept these contradictory ideas, we must investigate these stories of Enoch and Elijah.

A. ENOCH

So let us first look at the scriptures that tell us about Enoch. Genesis 5:23-24 says, "23Altogether, Enoch lived 365 years. 24Enoch walked with God; then he was no more, because God took him away." And Hebrews 11:5 says, 5By faith Enoch was taken *from this life,* so that he did not experience death; he could not be found, because God had taken him away. For before he was taken, he was commended as one who pleased God." Some today believe that the story of Enoch is about a man who lived faithfully in the

Lord and has been recognized as so in the eleventh chapter of Hebrews, and moreover, was blessed by God in that he was translated to heaven so that he would not die. It should be noted that even the translator of this version of the bible believed this since he added *from this life,* which does not appear in the Greek text.

1. A SPIRITUAL SENSE

In Hebrews 11:5 we first find the Greek word μετετέθη, which is in the passive tense meaning he was taken or was translated. Next we have the same Greek word but in the active sense and therefore spelled, μετέθηκεν, meaning took or translated. The first time this word is used, we are to understand it in a spiritual sense. John 5:24-25 speaks of a spiritual resurrection that is not universal. It is only referring to those who come to believe. The one who believes will metaphorically be crossed over, or translated, from death (the second death) to life (spiritual life in our present existence). This is the first resurrection referred to by many as being born again under the New Covenant. So this is what was meant with the first reference to Enoch being translated. It is to be taken figuratively to mean Enoch was translated so that he would not experience the second death. The only death that can be escaped according to Scripture is the second death, the lake of fire.

Here are some other scriptures to support this idea. This is what Jesus spoke of as mentioned in John 8:51 when Jesus said, "I tell you the truth, if anyone keeps my word, he will never see death [lit. for the eon]." With that said, the Jews questioned him by saying, "Abraham died and so did the prophets, yet you say that if anyone keeps your word, he will never taste death [lit. for the eon]." This is referring to the second death that occurs during the judgment eon or age for those in the resurrection to judgment at Christ's Second Coming. The same idea is in John 11:25-26 where Jesus is speaking to Martha. "Jesus said to her, 'I am the resurrection and the life.

He who believes in me will live [be resurrected], even though he dies; and whoever lives [is resurrected] and believes in me will never die [lit. for the eon].'" He apparently was again talking about the second death in the lake of fire during the judgment eon for unbelievers that can be escaped through believing in Jesus.

Let's look at what Paul says in Colossians 1:13. Speaking of Christ, he says, "For he has rescued us from the dominion of darkness and brought us into the kingdom of the Son he loves, in whom we have redemption, the forgiveness of sins." Here Paul speaks of a believer being figuratively translated into the kingdom of the Son. We, as Christians, are now figuratively in Christ's spiritual kingdom. At the Second Coming of Christ we will be given immortality and will be literally translated into the glorious kingdom on earth that will never end.

2. A GENERAL RESURRECTION

Here is another scripture that will make this plain. It is John 5:28-29. It reads, "Do not be amazed at this, for a time is coming when all who are in their graves will hear his voice and come out – those who have done good will rise to live, and those who have done evil will rise to be condemned [or judged]." This passage is universal, referring to all mankind. In other words, there will be at the Second Coming of Christ a general resurrection of all mankind. There will be a resurrection to life and a resurrection to judgment. This resurrection to judgment depicts the lake of fire that is symbolic of total destruction. Revelation 20:14 says that death and hades [the grave] are thrown into the lake of fire. These are abstract nouns and could not be thrown into a literal fire. The lake of fire is, therefore, symbolic of the total destruction of death and the grave. Fire is also a symbol of cleansing and this is where the spiritually dead will be judged and their sinful nature will be destroyed through loving chastisement and correction to bring them to the knowledge of the truth of the gospel (First Timothy 2:3-6; 4:10). God wants to bring about universal reconciliation to all mankind. There will be no more death, neither literal nor spiritual, once the sinful nature has been removed from all mankind during this judgment symbolized by the lake of fire.

3. DIED AFTER REMOVAL

Now the second reference to Enoch being translated is a literal translation, or transfer. Acts 7:16 tells us that the bodies of Jacob and his family who had died were carried (μετέτθησαν) to Shechem and placed in a tomb. Their bodies were transferred, or translated, to a new destination. So apparently men were trying to kill Enoch and God transferred him away to die elsewhere without being abused by attackers. This would be similar to what we were told about Moses's death. Deuteronomy 34:6 tells us that God took Moses away and that he died and was buried by God.

This understanding clears up the discrepancy some face, when they think Enoch did not die but instead was taken literally to heaven. Hebrews 11 says that all of these people listed, including Enoch, were still living by faith when they died. He like all human beings died and is waiting the general resurrection at the Second Coming of Christ.

B. ELIJAH

Now we need to look at scriptures regarding the life of Elijah and see if we can reconcile his account with what Jesus said about no one having ascended in heaven. Many today believe that Elijah was translated into heaven riding in a chariot. It says in Second Kings 2:11 that he was taken up in a whirlwind. One thing to notice in this verse is that when we talk of a whirlwind, we are talking about something that occurs in our atmosphere and not in outer space as would be the case if Elijah were transported to the third heaven where God sits on his throne.

The circumstance that this occurred in had to do with the fact that it was time for Elisha to replace Elijah as the prophet of God. In other words, it was time for Elijah to leave the scene and let Elisha be recognized by the people that God had appointed him to now be the one prophet of God for this time. There was now a new King of Israel, Jehoram. So with a new king, it was time for a new prophet.

Second Kings 2:11 tells us that Elijah was taken up in a whirlwind. This was not the first time that he had disappeared where no one could find him. In First Kings 18:7-17 we see that there were many occasions when King Ahab had sent men to many nations to find him and was unsuccessful. This disappearance of Elijah in a chariot was only the last time he had disappeared to another location where he could not be found. There are other cases in the Bible where God removed certain ones and transported them to a different location still on this earth. It should be noted that Ezekiel experienced being literally transported as we are told in Ezekiel 3:12-14. Also we have the story of Philip and the Ethiopian eunuch in Acts 8:26-23 and 39-40 in which we see that Philip was transported away to a different location after speaking with the Ethiopian eunuch.

We can know for sure the Elijah did not go in a whirlwind to the heavenly abode of God because a letter came about 10 years later from Elijah (Second Chronicles 21:12-15). The contents of it confirms that Elijah was alive and knew what had transpired since he left in that whirlwind. He mentioned that Jehoram had not followed the ways of his father Jehoshaphat but the wicked ways of the former kings of Israel and that he had murdered his brothers. These are the things that had been done after Elijah was taken away. Then in this letter he also speaks of the future. He warned that the LORD is about to strike Jehoram's people, his sons, his wives and everything he held dear. Then he also foretells that King Jehoram will become ill with a disease of the bowels and he will linger for a time before eventually dying by a rupture of the bowels. This should be evidence enough that Elijah was carried away to another location where he eventually died like everyone else does.

C. CONCLUSION

So with our study of Enoch and Elijah, we can again recall what is recorded of what Jesus said in John 3:13: "None has ever gone into heaven except the one who came from heaven – the Son of Man. Finally, with this insight on what happened in the lives of Enoch and Elijah, we should no longer see what appeared earlier to be a contradiction in Scripture.

CHAPTER 12:
DEATH IS A CURSE

S cripture says in Romans 6:23: "For the wages of sin is death, but the gift of God is eternal life in Christ Jesus our Lord." As Christians we believe that Christ came and lived a righteous life condemning sin in the flesh and paid for our sins by his death once and for all times. His death was for our sake so we can live again at the resurrection. He did not take away the curse of death at this time. The penalty remains but will be removed at his coming and we will then be given immortality to live forever in the Kingdom of Heaven that he will establish at that time.

A. Mortality passed to humanity because of Adam's sin

The penalty for Adam's sin was death, spiritually and eventually physically. He therefore was left mortal and not allowed to partake of the Tree of Life and gain immortality. Mortality was passed down to all of his descendants, not inherited sin. We are mortal and will die and without the second coming of Christ and the resurrection we would perish.

Yet most Christians today believe in a concept of the immortal soul. Adam was made of clay, or soil, and when God breathed his spirit into this man, Adam became a living soul, or an individual. Adam became a person like you and me, not an immortal soul residing within a body. Man is not a duality; he is one individual person made in the image of God. And God has predestined each individual, not his soul, to become in the image of Christ. And this will be done at the resurrection when Christ returns.

At Easter time the sermons that we hear are about Jesus dying to atone for our sins and that by believing what he has accomplished, we will be resurrected at his return so we can be in the kingdom with him. A few weeks later Christians are again saying that the gospel is about Jesus dying for our sins so that when we die we will immediately be in heaven with Jesus. Bible studies are usually given during the year to assure everyone that there is an intermediate state between death and the kingdom Christ will establish when he returns. All this is based on the false concept that Christians are immortal souls living in a physical body that eventually dies, but being immortal the individual continues life in another dimension. Yet First Corinthians 15 tells us that we are all dying and will perish without the resurrection that will come at the return of Christ. If we are going to perish than we cannot be immortal. First Corinthians 15 also tells us that when Christ returns he will resurrect the dead who are perishable and make them imperishable. He also promises to make the mortals immortal. One cannot become immortal if that one is already immortal; hence no one is immortal now but Jesus Christ who is the firstfruit of mankind. All others must wait for his return and the resurrection.

B. The dead are not immortal

First Timothy 6:14-16 says, "God only has immortality...." If God only has immortality then how can any of the dead be alive now? Christ died and was resurrected and made immortal and is the only human in heaven. There are no other humans who have died who are alive in heaven or hell today. Christ is the firstfruit of those who will be made alive at the Second

Coming. He is the only human who is immortal and has immortality to give at his Second Coming.

First Corinthians 15:53-54 says, at the Second Coming Christ will raise the dead imperishable and will change the mortal to immortality without dying. This is when humans will be made immortal, not before. This is when physical death will be swallowed up in victory. The dead are dead and the next moment of life will be at the resurrection when Christ returns as promised to rescue us from the penalty of death. Christ did not die in our place or we would not have to die. He died on our behalf atoning for our sins, leaving the death penalty in place for the time being. He will remove the death penalty at the Second Coming and save us from perishing by resurrecting dead individuals, not bodies. Christ will transform the lowliness of our body for it to be conformed to the body of his glory. First Corinthians 15:44 says that there are two bodies, a natural, or soul body (σῶυα ψυχικόν), and a spiritual body. We are sown as a natural body but raised as a spiritual body.

When one dies the spirit in man goes back to God who gave it (James 2:26 and Ecclesiastes 12:7) and can be used to create a new spiritual body of flesh and bone like the body Christ has in heaven. The dead are dead and their bodies decay and rot away. It would be impossible to reconstruct bodies that have commingled with other elements in the ground over the years becoming parts of other things.

Our hope, like Paul's (Phil. 3:20-21; Acts 23:6-9; 24:14-26, and 26:6-8), is in the resurrection to come at the Second Coming of Christ.

JOHN HUFFMAN

CHAPTER 13: ETERNAL TORMENT?

A. Punishment in hades or hell based on idea of justice

The topic of hades or hell should be discussed too, because, whether one believes in the immortal soul or not, many believe in the concept of reward and punishment. Many see the injustice in our world and think that there should be final justice, and the Scriptures say it will be exercised by Christ as the judge at the end of the world. Those who (it seems) have gotten away with all kinds of evil perpetrated on humanity, but never seemed to be dealt the justice they deserved in their lifetime, are thought to be called into account by Christ at the judgment at the end of the world (Second Peter 2:9). However, since Paul tells us, "God has bound all men over to disobedience so that he may have mercy on them all" (Romans 11:32), and since "God was reconciling the world [mankind] to himself in Christ, not counting men's sins against them" (Second Corinthians 5:19a), there seems to be hope for a favorable judgment at the end of the world to those who would take this opportunity at judgment to trust Christ for the salvation he has already provided (Second Corinthians 5:14-15).

As mentioned before by Lutzer and Grudem, it is believed that those unrighteous individual souls pass at their deaths into the tormenting side of hades. They will be tormented for their sins until the end of the world, when Christ returns and they are to be resurrected to have their souls and bodies once again reunited. It is at this time that Christ will judge them and have them cast into Gehenna, the lake of fire. This is a general description of the thought behind their beliefs in hades and Gehenna. Now let's look at what the Bible has to say about this.

The only mention of hell (Gehenna) outside of what Jesus is purported to have said about it in the Gospels is James 3:6 where it is in reference to the dangers of the tongue. The tongue corrupts the whole body and sets one's life on fire, and is set on fire itself by hell. There is no mention of Gehenna in the epistles of Paul, Peter, and John.

The messages of Gehenna were to the Jews only. Jesus came to Israel only. He was warning them of the upcoming judgment on them if they did not repent. Gehenna is a term that was in their background and therefore had meaning for them. If to the world then why did not Peter, Paul and John explain it in their epistles? Gentiles had no history to fall back on to understand his meaning. The term would not mean the same to them as it would to the Jews. The thing is that Gehenna should not be equated with hell in our Bibles either. Adam was not warned of a hell if he sinned by choosing the wrong tree. Cain was not warned of hell. If hell is real and should be avoided then mankind should have been warned long before Christ warned of Gehenna. Actually, Gehenna has simply been replaced as a word in theses scriptures with the word hell, which has a totally different meaning put in its place. This is not a translation; this is an interpretation.

Rob Bell summarizes the New Testament references to hades and Gehenna showing how little there is in the New Testament to support a belief in the everlasting torment of hell. He mentions where Jesus is quoted as referring to Gehenna in Matthew 5 and 23[104]. "In Matthew 10 and Luke 12 he [Jesus] says, 'Be afraid of the One who can destroy both soul and body in hell,' and in Matthew 18 and Mark 9 he says, 'It is better for you to enter life with one eye than to have]two eyes and be thrown into the fire of hell.'"[105] These are the only references to "hell" in the Bible.[106]

Bell says this about hades being mentioned in the Bible:

> Obscure, dark, murky – Hades is essentially the Greek version of the Hebrew word "Sheol." We find the word "Hades" in Revelation 1, 6, and 20 and in Acts 2, which is a quote from Psalm 16. Jesus uses the word in Matthew 11 and Luke 10: "You will go down to Hades"; in Matthew 16: "The gates of Hades will not overcome it"; and in the parable of the rich man and the beggar Lazarus in Luke 16.[107]

> Historically from the Old Testament, "Gehenna is a gorge that bends around the west and south sides of the Old or First Wall of Jerusalem like an L."[108] In Jeremiah 7:28-34, "Jeremiah plainly tells us what the valley symbolizes: he calls it 'the Valley of Slaughter'."[109]

Gehenna is the "English transliteration of the Greek form of an Aramaic word which in turn is derived from the Hebrew Phrase 'the Valley of [the son(s) of] Hinnom.'"[110] In the days of Ahaz and Manasseh, kings of Judah, this was the place for idolatry and the sacrificing of infants to the god

104 Rob Bell, *Love Wins* (New York: Harper One, 2001), 68.

105 Ibid.

106 Bell, 69.

107 Ibid.

108 Bradley Jersak, *Her Gates Will Never Be Shut: Hell, Hope, and the New Jerusalem* (Eugene, OR: Wipf and Stock, 2009), 34.

109 Ibid.

110 Walter A. Elwell, Gen. ed. *Baker Encyclopedia of the Bible,* anon., "Gehenna," vol. I. 2 vols. (Grand Rapids, MI Baker Book House, 1988), 844

Molech. Later, this valley became a place for depositing and burning refuse and even bodies of criminals.[111] When Jesus used *Gehenna*, he was using it metaphorically. He was giving a picture of how bad the effect of sin was on one's life. He was using this geographical place, known as a dumping area for garbage and even dead bodies of criminals, as a description of real experiences and consequences of living sinful lives in rebellion against God and his ways,[112] not some future life in another realm.

B. Unbelievers to be tormented in hell forever

Many say the Bible teaches eternal punishment for unbelievers. We know that believers have passed from death to life (John 5:24) and will at the resurrection enter their inheritance of the everlasting kingdom of God. Matthew 25:46 is the basic scripture from which this idea of eternal, or everlasting, punishment of the unbeliever comes from. According to Mounce, the Greek word κόλασιν (nominative form, κόλασις) can correctly be translated punishment, or chastisement, as in Matthew 25:46,[113] which could be disciplinary or corrective in nature. That would mean it is about teaching and correcting for the purpose of restoring those individuals to God's way of life for their possible deliverance into his kingdom.

In Acts 4:17-21 we have an example of κόλασις used with the idea of corrective punishment to persuade Peter and John to change their behavior. The rulers and elders wanted them to stop preaching and healing in the name of Jesus, but the leaders of the Sanhedrin were afraid of what the people's reaction might be. "Instead of responding to Peter's and John's statement of noncompliance with further prosecution [or corrective punishment], they're reduced to giving them only a further warning."[114]

111 Ibid.
112 Bell, 73.
113 Mounce, 286.
114 Gundry, 478

The Greek word αἰώνιον is the adjective form of αἰών, which means age, or "a period of time of significant character."[115] It does not mean eternal in the sense of time without any beginning or end. An age has a beginning and an end, whether we are aware of it or not. Only God is eternal and exists for all ages. In Matthew 25:46, the corrective punishment is αἰώνιον, meaning that it occurs during a period of time. Young translates Matthew 25:46 as, "And these shall go away to punishment age-during, but the righteous to life age-during."[116] Its duration is indefinite during the age to which it refers, but there will be a limit to its existence. The corrective punishment does not have to last the entire age, but until it has served its purpose. The Bible makes references to at least five ages (periods of time with a beginning and an end). If Christ had meant that unrighteous individuals would be sent into endless punishment, he could have used the Greek adjective ἀϊδίοις (*cidiois*), which Mounce defines as "always existing, eternal, Romans 1:20; Jude 6."[117] Besides, those who enter the Kingdom that Christ establishes at his return will be given immortality.

The final point is that if Gehenna was a place of endless torment, why did Paul not warn the Gentiles? Only in the Gospels do we see the Jews being warned of the Gehenna fire that would be unquenchable. Many biblical scholars, such as N.T. Wright, believe that Jesus' warning of Gehenna was a warning to the Jews of his generation regarding the coming judgment by fire to destroy Jerusalem, given to those who missed God's visitation to them in Jesus as God incarnate. Jesus warned them in Matthew 23 that the judgment on Jerusalem he was talking about would be in "this" generation, meaning his own. Wright remarks, "When Jesus was warning his hearers about Gehenna, he was not, as a general rule, telling them that unless they

115 Mounce, 57.
116 Young's Literal Translation.
117 Mounce, 55.

repented in this life they would burn in the next one."[118] The point Jesus was making was "Rome would turn Jerusalem into a hideous, stinking extension of its own smoldering rubbish heap. When Jesus said, 'Unless you repent, you will all likewise perish,' that is the primary meaning he had in mind."[119] It was not something that all mankind needed to be warned about through the gospel, or else Peter, Paul, and John would have certainly included it in their epistles.

118 N.T. Wright, *Surprised by Hope: Rethinking Heaven, the Resurrection, and the Mission of the* Church (New York: Harper One, 2008), 176.

119 Ibid.

CHAPTER 14: NO WARNING OF POSTMORTEM PUNISHMENT

Many have struggled with the idea taught in Catholic and Protestant churches regarding the teaching of postmortem eternal punishment in hell. Mankind was not warned of a postmortem punishment until the fourth century with Augustine's theology? Adam was warned that if he sinned, he would die that very day (Genesis 2:17), yet he actually lived to be 930 years old (Genesis 5:5). Therefore, he was not warned that the consequences of his sin would be an endless hell or eternal death as many teach. It was a moral, spiritual death that he experienced that day when he sinned. The death God threatened Adam with was in the day he sinned, in this life, not the hereafter. His physical death occurred later when his mortal body gave out since he had been left mortal because he sinned. He was made mortal from the dust or dirt of the earth and was denied access to the tree of life that would have given him eternal life (spiritual life) and eventually immortality.

This spiritual death, however, could be recovered. It was not the end for Adam nor was it for anyone else.[120] Ephesians 2:4-5 informs us, who are believers, that because of God's great love for us he made us alive (συνεζωοποίησεν) with Christ even when we were dead in transgressions. In First Corinthians 15:22, Paul uses the same Greek word to say that in Christ all will be made alive (ζωοποιηθήσονται), which is referring to the same "all" who in Adam died spiritually. This is about more than just a literal resurrection but also about a spiritual resurrection in Christ from spiritual death to spiritual life, which can occur in this life when we become believers or in the next age of judgment for unbelievers under Christ's direction and chastisement necessary to bring them to repentance and faith.

The penalty for Cain being the first murder was laid out to him, but nothing was mentioned about an ever burning hell to come after his death. His punishments for murder were all temporal and explained to him. How about the antediluvians? Noah preached and warned them of drowning. He never warned them of a post mortem hell of endless suffering.[121] Sodom and Gomorrah was about the punishment of a wicked people. They suffered fire and brimstone in this world, but they were not warned of endless punishment to await them at death, and there is no record that they ever experienced it.[122] God gave Moses the Law of commandments, statutes and judgments, but he never warned them of endless suffering in Hell if they failed to live up to these laws. Temporal punishments were handed out for disobedience, not hell.

In the Bible we have all of the nations of the earth living without any revelation from God of such a place. Pagans developed their own ideas

---

120 John Wesley Hanson, *Bible Proofs Of Universal Salvation: Containing The Principal Passages Of Scripture That Teach The Final Holiness And Happiness Of All Mankind*, 10th ed. (Boston: Universal Publishing House, 1903), 7.

121 Hanson, *Bible Proofs*, 9.

122 Hanson, *Bible Proofs*, 10.

of some kind of post mortem punishment to satisfy themselves that the wicked would eventually be punished, but they did not get these ideas from the God of the Bible. There is no record of anyone ever hearing a warning of hell in the four thousand years before Christ. We have to ask ourselves, would the gracious, merciful God of the Bible, who "… has bound all men over to disobedience so that he may have mercy on them all" (Romans 11:32) deliberately withhold the knowledge of the dire consequences of hell as the ultimate payment for sin? God has only said that the wages or penalty of sin is death, never hell.

The gospel of salvation is not about hell but about redemption from the penalty of sin, which is death. Christ redeemed us from spiritual death by his life of obedience free from sin and paid the penalty of physical death for us by his physical death. Through Christ's life, death and resurrection, God reconciled mankind to himself (Second Corinthians 5:17-19). We therefore, as this scripture continues saying, are called to be reconciled to God and then to witness to others telling them of this announcement so they too can come to believe that they also have already been reconciled by God and atoned for our sins through Christ and begin experiencing this newness of spiritual life in Christ.

CHAPTER 15: JESUS DID NOT WARN ABOUT HELL

The gospel is supposed to be good news, but is this what is really being disseminated today by good-hearted Christians in their personal witness to others and from the pulpits of many well-meaning churches? Many think the gospel message is to believe in Jesus and be saved from a hell of eternal torment. Peter said we should be willing to forgive a person seven times. Jesus then said we should be willing to forgive a person seventy times seven, in other words, an unlimited number of times. Jesus was actually describing God's grace and mercy to forgive us because he loves us. There is no deadline for his forgiveness. His love and mercy never fails, but we have to accept his forgiveness through Jesus and the life he gave to remove the curse resulting from sin, which is death (Romans 6:23), not hell.

Much of our misunderstanding regarding the concept of eternal torment in hell after the death of an unsaved person is due to misunderstanding the original words IN Greek and Hebrew that have been co-opted by the replacement of the word *hell* in the gospels. So first, let's look at these words and their original meanings and how replacing them with the word *hell* with all of its pagan baggage and meaning has corrupted the gospel message and has marred our picture of God who loves the world (John 3:16, 17) and wants all men to be saved and come to a knowledge of the truth (First Timothy 2:4).

Secondly, in this chapter we will also look at the words that Jesus is remembered for saying to the Jews to warn them of a coming judgment on Judea and Jerusalem. We will see that what Jesus is remembered in the gospels for saying regarding judgment was only spoken to the Jews of Judea and Jerusalem. He said that he came to Israel only and therefore not to the Gentiles. This is why Peter, Paul and John never mentioned these same words of Jesus in their epistles for the world to read.

A. HELL – SHEOL, HADES, GEHENNA

We want to begin in this chapter by defining the three words: Sheol, Hades and genhenna as used by Jesus. *Sheol* is the place of the dead in which both the good and the bad go when they die. It simply means the grave and many of the Old Testament texts that contain the word *sheol* clearly can only mean the grave. *Sheol* in the Septuagint Greek translation of the Old Testament is translated by the Greek word *hades*.

Hades also appears in the Greek text of the New Testament and is another word for which translators insert the word *hell*. Almost universally hades has been taught to be the "intermediate state" between death and resurrection in which it is supposedly divided into two parts, one for the godly of the Old Testament and the other for the ungodly or lost.

The word most frequently used (occurring twelve times) in the New Testament that is thought of by many as referring to the place of future punishment is *gehenna*. *Gehenna* originally referred to the Valley of Hinnom, south and west of Jerusalem. A place in the valley called Topheth is remembered as the location of Baal worship and the sacrificing of children to Molech.[123] Later this valley became a garbage dump where filth, dead animals and bodies of criminals were tossed into it and burned up. Its fires were kept burning to consume the debris that was continually being cast into it and to prevent disease. It gained the connotation of whatever was tossed into it was condemned, corrupt, or useless. Jesus began using it metaphorically as a symbol of national judgment. Israel had been corrupted by its leaders and he was warning the nation that judgment was coming if they did not repent.

Clement of Alexandria (185-254 A.D.) and Justin Martyr (150-195 A.D) were the first to write that Gehenna was a place of punishment after death. Clement was a Universalist, believing that all mankind would eventually be saved through belief in Christ, and therefore did not say this punishment was endless. It is unclear whether Martyr believed it to be temporal or endless.[124] It is also important to note that endless punishment after death is not mentioned in the Apostles' Creed or the Nicene Creed from the 4th century A.D. The idea of endless punishment after death came later.

Paul Kurts explains:

> It wasn't until the time of St. Augustine of Hippo (c. 354-430) and St. Jerome (c. 347-420) that the concept [of endless punishment] they borrowed from Plato (429-47 B.C.E.) was put into Catholic doctrine when Jerome by order of Pope Damasus, translated the **Latin Vulgate** from earlier Latin and Greek Scriptures from 382 to 405 A.D.[125]

With the Scriptures in Latin and only the priests being able to read them, the Roman Catholic Church had great power and control over its members by fear of excommunication. This situation was greatly changed with

123

124 T. A. Herring, *Scandalous Grace: Rediscovering the truth of God's unconditional love, mercy, forgiveness and grace for all people* (Lavergne, TN: T. A. Herring, 2014), 73.

125 Paul Kurts, *Hell Letters: Exposing the Myth* (Bloomington, IN: WestBow Press, 2013), 11.

the emergence of Martin Luther and the Protestant Reformation in 1517. The Reformation provided alternate churches, yet they too unfortunately continued this same doctrine of eternal punishment after death as a means to control their members too.[126]

We will now need to look at how various words in Scripture have been employed to paint a picture of a hell of doom for the majority of humanity, but along with this we will explain how these verses applied to Jesus' generation and not to any punishment after death.

B. VERSES CONTAINING *GEHENNA*

1. MATTHEW 5:21-22:

> [21] "You have heard that it was said to the people long ago, 'You shall not murder, and anyone who murders will be subject to judgment.' [22] But I tell you that anyone who is angry with a brother or sister[j] will be subject to judgment. Again, anyone who says to a brother or sister, 'Raca,' is answerable to the court. And anyone who says, 'You fool!' will be in danger of the fire of hell.

The Greek word for judgment here is *krisis* which means judgment or a court of 7 men set up in several cities of Palestine to make judgments on cases involving individuals. The word *raca* means empty head, which would imply stupid. The English word *council* refers to the Sanhedrin of 70 men, making up the superior court of the land and located in Jerusalem. The Greek word *mora*, here translated fool, could be the transliteration of the Aramaic word *mora* which means rebel and is the way it is translated in Young's Literal Translation. *Rebel* makes more sense since there would not be much of a distinction between an empty head and a fool, but rebel would give more comprehension to the idea of one ending up in *gehenna*.

---

126 Kalen Fristad, *Destined For Salvation: God's Promise to Save Everyone* (Kearney, NE: Morris Publishing, 1997), 68, 69.

The word, *gehenna*, is a transliteration of the Valley of Hinnom, which became a dumping ground for rebels whom the Roman government crucified. Israel, led by the leadership in Jerusalem, was an apostate nation of rebels. Jesus used this term, *gehenna*, metaphorically as a warning to those who would not heed his message of the coming kingdom of heaven (or God) and repent. It was an apostate nation of rebels.

2. MATTHEW 5:29-30:

> [29] If your right eye causes you to stumble, gouge it out and throw it away. It is better for you to lose one part of your body than for your whole body to be thrown into hell [gehenna, metaphorical of the destruction of Jerusalem]. [30] And if your right hand causes you to stumble, cut it off and throw it away. It is better for you to lose one part of your body than for your whole body to go into hell [gehenna].

This is another record of Jesus warning against national judgment using the metaphorical expression of *gehenna*, of which the translators again inserted their choice of the word "hell." Jesus was making the point that it is better to go into the soon coming Messianic kingdom (the church age) than into the imminent national judgment of unquenchable fire with all their present members. Those who received his message watched for the sign he gave them to know when the desolation of Jerusalem was near, and they were able to escape to Pella and surrounding areas. (Mark 13:14; Luke 21:20-21).

3. MATTHEW 10:28:

> [28] Do not be afraid of those who kill the body but cannot kill the soul. Rather, be afraid of the One who can destroy both soul and body in hell [gehenna].

God is capable of destroying the whole person in the Gehenna destruction of Jerusalem. He *could* destroy it so that they would never live again if he chose to do so. Jesus told the Pharisees in Matthew 3:9, ". . . do not think you can say to yourselves, 'we have Abraham as our father.' I tell you that out of these stones God can raise up children for Abraham." So Jesus said God could raise up stones to praise him, but he didn't. God will not destroy both soul and body forever because Scripture indicates that all will be resurrected when Christ returns, and according to First Corinthians 15:26 Christ will ultimately destroy death, not anyone's body and soul (life) permanently.

4. LUKE 12:5

⁵ But I will show you whom you should fear: Fear him who, after your body has been killed, has authority to throw you into hell. Yes, I tell you, fear him.

This is saying that God could cast their dead bodies into Gehenna, a reference to the garbage pit where fires were kept burning to keep down disease and destroy what was unwanted. This is not talking of an after-death judgment, but in reference to this soon coming literal judgment on apostate Israel. Bodies of criminals and persons who had died with no one claiming them as loved ones or belonging to a family were cast into this garbage dump. It was a shameful end for a person's body to be cast into Gehenna. The Jewish leaders represented this evil generation on which was the blood of the prophets. God's vengeance would be required of this generation (Luke 11:50-51) and warned the people against the leaven of the Pharisees (Luke 12:1).

5. MATTHEW 18:8-9:

⁸ If your hand or your foot causes you to stumble, cut it off and throw it away. It is better for you to enter life maimed or crippled than to have two hands or two feet and be thrown into eternal fire. ⁹ And if your eye causes you to stumble, gouge it out and throw it away. It is better for you to enter life with one

eye than to have two eyes and be thrown into the fire of hell [gehenna fire].

The literal Greek words translated "eternal fire" here is αἰώνιος πῦρ (*aiōnios fire*). The Greek word αἰώνιος is the adjective form of the noun, *aiōv*, which means an age that has a beginning and an end. An adjective can never mean more than its noun form. So the adjective form would mean, of or pertaining to an age. And therefore, this verse is not referring to an eternal fire.

Fire is often used in Scripture as a metaphor for national judgment. This fire mentioned here is the national judgment pertaining to the coming end of the Jewish age. Jesus was warning of the fiery judgment to come on Jerusalem, which did occur forty years later.

Also note that the word "hell" was inserted by translators, though it does not translate the Greek word, *gehenna*. It replaced *gehenna* and its meaning with an entirely new meaning, which amounted to an interpretation rather than a translation. This practice is repeated in the other verses in which Jesus mentioned gehenna.

6. MATTHEW 23:15, 33, 36:

[15] "Woe to you, teachers of the law and Pharisees, you hypocrites! You travel over land and sea to win a single convert, and when you have succeeded, you make them twice as much a child of hell as you are. [33] "You snakes! You brood of vipers! How will you escape being condemned to hell? [36] Truly I tell you, all this will come on this generation.

He condemned strongly the scribes and Pharisees' unworthy, unacceptable laxity of their spiritual condition and was telling them that by proselyting others they were drawing these new converts into this same wretched spiritual condition they had that opposed God. Jesus, knowing their spiritual condition, asked how they expected to escape the Gehenna judgment coming on Jerusalem in this generation in which they were living.

7. MARK 9:43-48:

> [43] If your hand causes you to stumble, cut it off. It is better for you to enter life maimed than with two hands to go into hell [gehenna], where the fire never goes out." [45] And if your foot causes you to stumble, cut it off. It is better for you to enter life crippled than to have two feet and be thrown into hell [gehenna]." [47] And if your eye causes you to stumble, pluck it out. It is better for you to enter the kingdom of God with one eye than to have two eyes and be thrown into hell [gehenna], [48] where "'the worms that eat them do not die, and the fire is not quenched.

The mentioning of gehenna in these verses are references to the fiery judgment coming on Jerusalem if they did not repent and accept him as their messiah. Jesus was warning them that it was better to go into the messianic kingdom (church age) that was coming missing body parts than into the imminent national judgment of unquenchable fire with all their present members.

8. JAMES 3:6:

> [6] The tongue also is a fire, a world of evil among the parts of the body. It corrupts the whole body, sets the whole course of one's life on fire, and is itself set on fire by hell [gehenna].

James is warning about gossip, which can be hurtful. Literally *Gehenna* is used here as a figure representing unpleasant, impure and hurtful thoughts very much like garbage and not worthy of passing on.

C· VERSES CONTAINING *HADES*

1. LUKE 10:13-15 (See also Matthew 11:20-24; 12:41-42; and Luke 11:29-32):

> [13] "Woe to you, Chorazin! Woe to you, Bethsaida! For if the miracles that were performed in you had been performed in Tyre and Sidon, they would have repented long ago, sitting in sackcloth and ashes. [14] But it will be more bearable for Tyre and Sidon at the judgment than for you. [15] And you, Capernaum, will you be lifted to the heavens? No, you will go down to <u>Hades</u>. . . ."

Jesus is saying that though Capernaum thought it was favored by heaven (God), now they will be thrust down as if to hades (the grave) with the utmost indignation and shame to themselves.

Jesus was shaming the unbelieving Jews. The shame was based solely upon Jesus' knowledge that those who were regarded as object lessons for immorality (i.e. Sodom and Gomorrah, Tyre and Sidon), under similar circumstances of experiencing Jesus' ministry, would have done better than what the unbelieving Jews did.

2. MATTHEW 16:18:

> [18] "And I tell you that you are Peter, and on this rock I will build my church, and the gates of Hades [the grave] will not overcome it."

The gospel is the good news announcement to be proclaimed by the church about the universal reconciliation (Second Corinthians 5:18, 19) and eventual resurrection of all mankind through Jesus. Jesus is saying that no power can prevent the dead from being resurrected from their graves when the time comes. This is a promise that death will not always be present. Other scriptures tell us that death and hades will be destroyed (Revelation 20:14) and death will be no more (Revelation 21:4). Death will not prevail against the message of the church but will ultimately be destroyed itself.

3. LUKE 16:23:

²³"In Hades, where he was in torment, he looked up and saw Abraham far away, with Lazarus by his side."

This is an intriguing verse and surrounding context that will require a lengthy explanation and more than we should cover in this section. Please follow this passage up in the next chapter titled, "The Parable of Lazarus and the Rich Man." We will give a full exegesis of the entire passage there.

4. ACTS 2:25-28:

²⁵ David said about him [Christ]:"'I [Christ] saw the Lord [God, the Father] always before me [Christ]. Because he is at my [Christ] right hand, I [Christ] will not be shaken. ²⁶ Therefore my Christ's] heart is glad and my [Christ's] tongue rejoices; my [Christ's] body also will rest in hope, ²⁷ because you [God] will not abandon me [Christ] to the realm of the dead, you [God] will not let your holy one [Christ] see decay. ²⁸ You have made known to me [Christ] the paths of life; you will fill me [Christ] with joy in your presence.

Peter says here that this is a prophecy by David about Jesus, the Christ, and his promised resurrection (v29) because he was not abandoned to the grave (*hades*) in verse 31. Peter also says, however, that David died and was buried and is still in his tomb (not resurrected) and has not ascended to heaven (as an immortal soul).

5. REVELATION 1:18:

¹⁸ I am the Living One; I was dead, and now look, I am alive for ever and ever! And I hold the keys of death and Hades [the grave]."

Christ was raised from the dead and has the keys of authority and power to break the hold of death and raise humanity from the grave at the Second Coming.

6. REVELATION 6:8:

⁸ I looked, and there before me was a pale horse! Its rider was named Death, and Hades [the grave] was following close behind him. They were given power over a fourth of the earth [land] to kill by sword, famine and plague, and by the wild beasts of the earth [land].

This judgment would bring about much death and the need for many graves to bury the dead. The word translated as "earth" can also be translated as "land" depending on the context. The context is about the land of Judea where Jerusalem was located.

D. VERSES CONTAINING *FIRE*

1. MATTHEW 3:12 (& Luke 3:17):

¹² "His winnowing fork is in his hand, and he will clear his threshing floor, gathering his wheat into the barn and burning up the chaff with unquenchable fire."

John the Baptist forewarned the Jews about Jesus and the judgment of God, which Christ was ready to execute on the unbelieving and impenitent Jews. By using the Greek word ἄσβεστος *(asbestos),* he was foretelling them that no one would be able to put out the fire or stop it when it came.

2. MATTHEW 13:50:

⁵⁰ "and throw them into the blazing furnace [destruction of Jerusalem], where there will be weeping and gnashing of teeth."

Again, this was a metaphor of the judgment and destruction that would come on Jerusalem unless it repented.

3. MATTHEW 25:41:

⁴¹ "Then he will say to those on his left, 'Depart from me, you who are cursed, into the eternal fire prepared for the devil and his angels."

The words "eternal fire" here is rendered from the Greek words αἰόνιος πῦρ, which literally mean age-during fire, in other words pertaining to the age. It represents the quality of fire, not its duration. The metaphor of fire here is of an indeterminate period of time. This is age-during fire of national judgment to be brought upon Judea, and specifically Jerusalem.

The reference to the devil and his angels is probably figurative, rather than literal. The word devil can be employed as a metaphor for those who oppose God and therefore seem to act the part of the devil. In this instance it could be referring to the high priest and other prominent leaders of Jerusalem who opposed Jesus and his message of the coming kingdom of God. John 6:70 is an example where Jesus used this word as a metaphor when he referred to Judas as a devil.

4. REVELATION 20:10:

[10] "And the devil, who deceived them, was thrown into the lake of burning sulfur, where the beast and the false prophet had been thrown. They will be tormented day and night for ever and ever."

This occurs at the end of the church age and refers to the utter defeat and destruction of what the devil has effortlessly worked to accomplish. The symbolic beast and false prophet, who represented the persecuting Roman government and the corrupting false religion of Judea had earlier, according to Revelation 19:20, been cast into this lake of fire symbolizing their utter defeat and destruction. The Roman emperor, Nero, and the high priest both died around the same time as the destruction of Jerusalem. Despite what is usually taught today, what the beast and the false prophet symbolize was in the past, not something to come in our future.

The beast from the sea was a symbol for the Roman Empire corporately and Nero particularly. The second beast was from the land. The land here would be that of Judea and so the false prophet was the symbol for the apostate Jews, the Jewish High Priestly aristocracy of Jerusalem. The beast and the false prophet were figuratively thrown into the lake of fire destroying what they had built for themselves.

The first part of this verse, "And the devil, who deceived them, was thrown into the lake of burning sulfur, where the beast and the false prophet had been thrown," is a parenthetical clause, and the second part saying, "they will be tormented day and night forever and ever [lit. Grk. is ages of ages] refers to the nations of people in the foregoing verses. They, the people, will be tormented for however long it takes to bring about their utter defeat and destruction. These three symbols are abstractions and cannot be tormented. The phrase *ages of ages* does not mean without end, but that it will continue as long as it is needed to accomplish God's judgment on them even through a judgment age.

5. REVELATION 20:14-15

[14] "Then death and Hades were thrown into the lake of fire. The lake of fire is the second death. [15] Anyone whose name was not found written in the book of life was thrown into the lake of fire."

Generally speaking death and the grave are figuratively thrown into the lake of fire, which is a symbol of utter defeat and destruction. In other words, there will no longer be physical death and graves in which to bury them. Those whose names are not in the book of life will be thrown into this lake of fire not to punish or destroy them but to change them. Revelation 21:8 lists categories of those who will be consigned to this lake of fire and brimstone.

Romans 6:3-4 explains that believers died with Christ and were raised to a new spiritual life (a moral resurrection). This was the first death and resurrection experienced by believers (John 5:24-25) and were promised that they would not be subject to the second death (Revelation 20:6). Verses 14 and 15 above are about those who will be subject to the second death spiritually speaking in the literal resurrection to judgment so that they too can be raised spiritually (a moral resurrection) to a new converted life in Christ.

The spiritually dead (unsaved) will have their fallen nature destroyed. Brimstone, or Sulphur, here is a symbol of a cleaning agent and fire symbolically represents a process of change. Fire never destroys but only converts or changes one substance to another. God is a consuming fire desiring a spiritual change in us. These spiritually dead persons will be going through a process that may feel like torment but it will be for the purpose of transforming their carnal minds to spiritual minds. Once converted to Christ they then will enter the kingdom as God's adopted sons and daughters as believers are now. Our Triune God's overall plan is one of restoration of all of fallen humanity to a true spiritual relationship and fellowship with the Father, Son and Holy Spirit.

E. VERSES CONTAINING *DARKNESS* AND *GNASHING OF TEETH*

1. MATTHEW 8:11-12:

> [11] I say to you that many will come from the east and the west, and will take their places at the feast with Abraham, Isaac and Jacob in the kingdom of heaven. [12] But the subjects of the kingdom will be thrown outside, into the darkness, where there will be weeping and gnashing of teeth.

Dealing with the faith of the centurion, Jesus said that converts will come from all over into the kingdom, and will figuratively sit at the table with Abraham, Isaac and Jacob, the forefathers of the Jews, while the children of the kingdom (the Jews) will be thrown outside (having not come to believe yet) into darkness and there will be gnashing of teeth. This kingdom cannot be referring to the kingdom of the immortal state because the children of that kingdom will never be cast out.[127] The gnashing of teeth would be referring to their reaction to the great tribulation that will be soon coming on them for rejecting Jesus as the Christ. Jesus is saying that the sons of the kingdom, these Jews of Jesus' generation who were rejecting him, will be cast out into outer darkness, meaning the Gentile world, with its blindness and darkness of mind. The weeping and gnashing of teeth would be their angry response.

2. MATTHEW 22:13:

[13]"Then the king told the attendants, 'Tie him hand and foot, and throw him outside, into the darkness, where there will be weeping and gnashing of teeth.'"

This is the parable of the wedding garment. This person did not come in wearing the garment of faith and righteousness received only from Christ, but wearing his filthy rags of his own righteousness. This was tantamount to being a thief and must, in the parable, be bound hand and foot to denote the greatness of his crime. The weeping and gnashing of teeth would be his response to being cast out.

The wedding garment portrays the coming marriage of Christ with his followers who will become the church at Pentecost, without these Jewish leaders who rejected Jesus' invitation to follow him and be spared this national judgment.

3. LUKE 13:28-30:

[28]"There will be weeping there, and gnashing of teeth, when you see Abraham, Isaac and Jacob and all the prophets in the kingdom of God, but you yourselves thrown out. [29]People will come from east and west and north and south, and will take their places at the feast in the kingdom of God. [30]Indeed there are

---

127 Thomas Baldwin Thayer, *Theology Of Universalism: Being An Exposition Of Its Doctrines And Teachings, In Their Logical And Moral Relations* (Boston: Universalist Publishing House, 1891), 377, 378.

those who are last who will be first, and first [Jews] who will
be last."

All Israel was called first, but few answered the call becoming the
chosen of spiritual Israel. At Christ's spiritual coming in judgment (at the
end of the Jewish age) there would be a separation between those who have
come to believe in Christ and those who have not. Those who have not will
have to suffer in the destruction of Judea and Jerusalem.

Figuratively, Abraham, Isaac and Jacob and all the prophets representing
the Jews who did accept Jesus as the Christ will be enjoying the kingdom
together as Christian followers of Christ in the church age that would begin
at Pentecost.

Unless they repent and come to Christ is this life, they will go through
an age of judgment beginning at the resurrection for as long as it takes to
come to faith in Christ. In due time, it is hoped that they will be able to enter
the glorious kingdom prepared for them too. Those who come to believe
in this age will recline at the table (eucharist) in the messianic kingdom
(church age).

4. MATTHEW 25:30:

[30] "Throw out the worthless slave into the outer darkness; in
that place there will be weeping and gnashing of teeth."

This is the parable of the talents. The master had given his servants
talents to use in his absence (depicting the time between his ascension and
his spiritual coming in judgment on Jerusalem) and this one hid his. He was
unfaithful and not profitable while his master was gone and so he would
be thrown out into the darkness with others who were not profitable either.
And there was weeping and gnashing of teeth bewailing his miserable
condition.

F. VERSE CONTAINING THE IDEAS OF SEPARATION AND TORMENT

WHY BELIEVE IT?
AN ARGUMENT AGAINST THE TEACHINGS OF THE IMMORTAL SOUL

1. MATTHEW 7:23:

²³ Then I will tell them plainly, 'I never knew you. Away from me, you evildoers!'

"I never knew you," was a hyperbole. He meant that he never had a relationship with them because they never knew him, that is, who he was.

2. SECOND THESSALONIANS. 1:9:

⁹ "These will pay the penalty of eternal destruction, away from the presence of the Lord and from the glory of His power, ..."

"Eternal destruction" in this verse is the translation of the Greek words, αἰώνιος ὄλεθρος (*aiōnios olethros*). To be able to understand how these words are used, one needs to read verses 3-10 noting that the pronouns "you" and "us," are referring to the first century believers including Paul and fellow workers.

Paul says that God will trouble those who trouble these first century Christians and thereby give them and him and his fellow workers relief from the persecutions they are enduring. In the context this destruction is not descriptive of a separation nor a destruction occurring after one dies, but of what is to occur to those in the first century who are persecuting these Christians.

3. REVELATION 14:9-11:

⁹ A third angel followed them and said in a loud voice: "If anyone worships the beast and its image and receives its mark on their fore head or on their hand, ¹⁰ they, too, will drink the wine of God's fury, which has been poured full strength into the cup of his wrath. They will be tormented with burning sulfur in the presence of the holy angels and of the Lamb. ¹¹ And the smoke of their torment will rise for ever and ever [to the ages of ages]. There will be no rest day or night for those who worship

the beast and its image, or for anyone who receives the mark of its name."

This is about God's wrath on those worshipping the beast on earth. It was not about an after death experience. The lamb is merely present and they are being tormented because of the condition within their own minds. They feel condemned by their own consciences. They are under deep conviction but are still resisting what they know deep down in their hearts is true.

God's glory is as a lake of fire and brimstone to the sinner who has not repented and come to the ever-loving Savior for forgiveness and reconciliation. For him it is not over when this life ends. There will be a resurrection to judgment (John 5:28-29) wherein he continues to experience this inner feeling of the torment of the lake of fire and brimstone continually until the change is made. This lake of fire and brimstone is not a literal fire of unending torture, but God's glory as a consuming fire that will cleanse, purge and purify the sinner. Those in the resurrection to judgment will experience profound conviction and will be tormented by it, having no rest, until they finally yield to the presence of the Lamb who loves them. When that happens there will be tears and weeping of joy and relief, as hopefully every knee will eventually bow to Christ, their Savior and Lord.

G. VERSES CONTAINING THE IDEA OF JUDGMENT

1. SECOND PETER 2:4:

4"For if God did not spare angels when they sinned, but sent them to hell [ταρταρόω, tartaroō], putting them in chains of darkness to be held for judgment; . . . . "

"*Hell* here is a Greek concept (see RSV mg.) and refers in Greek mythology to Tartarus, the lowest and most terrible part of hell, reserved especially for those superhuman beings that rebelled against the supreme God."[128] "The imagery appears to be drawn from apocryphal writings."[129]

Peter is not talking about humans being in hell, but rather uses this Greek word as a way of explaining the imprisonment of the angels who fell because of their sin and are to be restrained on earth until the judgment.[130]

2. MATTHEW 13:47-50:

[47]Once again, the kingdom of heaven is like a net that was let down into the lake and caught all kinds of fish. [48] When it was full, the fishermen pulled it up on the shore. Then they sat down and collected the good fish in baskets, but threw the bad away. [49] This is how it will be at the end of the age. The angels will come and separate the wicked from the righteous [50] and throw them into the blazing furnace, where there will be weeping and gnashing of teeth.

This is a judgment parable much like the judgment parable of the sheep and goats in Matthew 25. It is about the warning of a coming separation of those who received Jesus' message of the soon coming kingdom of God and those rebel Jews who rejected his message and even plotted to kill him. Eventually they were the ones responsible for pressuring the crowds to call for Jesus' crucifixion.

3. MATTHEW 25:46:

[46] "Then they will go away to eternal punishment, but the righteous to eternal life."

The phrase "eternal punishment" in this verse is a translation of the Greek words, $\alpha i\acute{\omega}\nu\iota o\varsigma$ $\kappa\acute{o}\lambda\alpha\sigma\iota\varsigma$. These words literally mean age-during chastisement, or chastisement pertaining to the age. The word $\kappa\acute{\epsilon}\lambda\alpha\sigma\iota\varsigma$

---

128 Guthrie and Motyer, 1255.

129 Ibid.

130 Paul Kurts, *Trinitarian Letters: Your Adoption And Inclusion In The Life Of God* (Bloomington, IN: WestBow Press, 2011), 194.

originally referred to pruning trees to make them grow. This chastisement then is for the purpose of making the recipient a better person. That is God's purpose according to many scriptures, but he works this out in his own time.

This passage is about judgment in this 25th chapter of Matthew, and it pertains to the judgment on Jerusalem at the end of the Jewish age. Jerusalem was to be destroyed within the generation of Jews that Jesus was personally speaking to, which did occur within the next 40 years, in A.D. 70. Even though the inhabitants of Jerusalem, who had rejected Jesus as the Christ, would be killed or captured and enslaved at that time, they will have been chastised and will be resurrected to judgment at the Second Coming of Christ in the future wherein their chastisement will continue until they come to repentance and acceptance of Christ.

The righteous are those Jesus has described by their good deeds as having become his disciples in general. They would become the church that was to be established at Pentecost. They, as believers in Christ, were given eternal life. This is the same eternal life that we, as believers in the church have today. Eternal, or *aionian* life, is not immortal life, but the kind or quality of life we have as adopted sons and daughters of God. We have been adopted by the Father through the Son by the Holy Spirit. John 17:3 describes this spiritual relationship, termed eternal life that we have with our Triune God in Jesus.

4. JUDE 6:

> [6] "And the angels who did not keep their positions of authority but abandoned their proper dwelling—these he has kept in darkness, bound with everlasting chains for judgment on the great Day.

This Greek word, ἀΐδιος, in the phrase, "in everlasting *(ἀΐδιος, aïdios)* chains until judgment day," actually does mean eternal or everlasting, but the duration here is qualified to come to an end at the judgment. So this is not even about lasting eternally.

H. CONCLUSION

It is clear from the terms actually used in Scripture as opposed to the word *hell* that has been imposed on Scripture through translators that the Bible does not proclaim a gospel that threatens compliance, or suffer the consequences of a fiery hell of eternal misery and torment as punishment from God for our sins in this life. What people picture hell to be like comes from paganism, not the Holy Word of God. God in Christ has redeemed all mankind from their sins in this life, but God wants all to accept Christ's sacrifice and pass from spiritual death to spiritual life in Christ. For those not doing this in this life, they will have an opportunity at the judgment before Jesus the Judge "who is the Savior of all mankind, and especially of those who believe" (First Timothy 4:10).

CHAPTER 16: ORTHODOX POSITION REGARDING THE PURPOSE OF THE RESURRECTION

A. The nature of God and how it contributes to the issue

Our Triune God's nature is one of love for the humanity he created. God does not want to "get even" with mankind for its sins against him. "God demonstrates his own love for us in this: While we were still sinners, Christ died for us" (Romans 5:8). He does not want to punish sinners forever, but rather "wants all men to be saved and to come to a knowledge of the truth" (First Timothy 2:4). Man has been given the gospel of what God in Christ has accomplished for man's salvation, but each person has a choice whether to respond to his gift of grace and salvation. Scripture does not reveal whether all mankind, whom Christ died for, will respond to his drawing (John 12:32). God's method of dealing with sin is revealed in the gospel as desiring reconciliation. It involves "setting people right with God and with one another," rather than seeking to punish them (as they most certainly deserve) to bring about justice. This is God's display of his grace.[131]

---

131 Michael J. Gorman, *Reading Paul* (Milton Keynes, U.K.: Paternoster, 2008), 120.

God recognizes the present evil in the world and intends to make a perfect world in which his desire will be done on earth as it is in heaven. He desires healing, not destruction of the world of mankind. The power of evil has been defeated at the cross, and he will bring healing to the nations through the redeemed. They will be the stewards of his new creation. God's love and redemptive activity is being proclaimed to the world now through those who have voluntarily become his servants trusting in their redemption accomplished in Christ while they were yet sinners and enemies with God (Romans 5:8).[132]

Penal justice is involved traditionally with the immortal soul concept, and it is even believed by some universalists, whereby it will eventually bring all to accept God's salvation. However, God's justice is through Christ, as our Mediator, bringing reconciliation between God and man. Second Corinthians 5:18-20 reads,

> All this is from God, who reconciled us to himself through Christ and gave us the ministry of reconciliation: that God was reconciling the world to himself in Christ, not counting men's sins against them. And he has committed to us the message of reconciliation. We are therefore Christ's ambassadors as though God were making his appeal through us. We implore you on Christ's behalf: Be reconciled to God.

But those who hold to the immortal soul traditionally believe that every person must be judged for the things they have done in this life. Those in hades will be cast into hell (Gehenna) to suffer eternally for their sins.[133] No one will be saved by their works, but those who have not accepted Christ's

132 N.T. Wright, *Evil and the Justice of God* (Downers Grove, IL: InterVarsity Press, 2006), 141.

133 Lutzer, 109.

sacrifice for their sins, we are told, will be judged by their works and deeds done in this life. Their life will be minutely analyzed for whatever thoughts and ill motives they have had. All unbelievers will be found guilty.[134] Penal justice says that someone must pay for everything that has been done wrong. He must pay for his sins against God, unless he has accepted Christ's sacrifice for his sins. In God's grace, his only Son, Jesus, died for our sake by paying the debt of death for sins.

When one believes in the immortal soul, he believes that the soul leaves the body at death and will go to hades if he has not accepted the gospel. He will remain there until the coming of Christ and the final judgment, which will then send him to *Gehenna*, which they believe will be the lake of fire, and torment for that individual forever. At the resurrection this individual will receive an indestructible body, so it will not be consumed in the lake of fire but will remain in excruciating pain and torment forever.[135]

Jesus, the incarnate Son of God, showed his love for mankind in that he, although innocent, died for the sins of humanity (First John 2:2) and had to be resurrected to bring us life according to Scripture.

Pagans believed that the soul of man continued to exist past the death of the body, based on their philosophy and reason. "They had, as we know, some vague hopes and longings for immortality in another world."[136] "They pictured forth according to their imaginings as to what might and ought to be, but they knew nothing of resurrection from the dead."[137] They didn't believe in Jesus as their Savior, or that this life of the soul was given to them by God. They believed that the soul was innately immortal. They believed it resided within them, and they had no need for it to be supplied to them by a deity.

134 Ibid.
135 Ibid., 116.
136 Spencer, 58.
137 Ibid., 59.

The immortal soul concept assumes an ongoing life, whether in heaven, hell, or limbo, without the need of Jesus' death and resurrection. The Christian message, however, brings to light that there exists God, the Creator of life and the universe, and it is he who must bestow immortality, since he only has immortality innately (First Timothy 6:13-16). The gospel informs us that it is God's plan to bring about immortality for mankind, but it is through the life, death, resurrection and ascension of his Son, Jesus Christ. Jesus, the Son of God incarnate, was without sin, having sanctified the sinful nature of man throughout his life on earth, and then willingly gave his perfect human life for the sake of mankind, he qualified mankind for the gift of immortality—a gift that Scripture indicates is given only at the resurrection (1 Corinthians 15:53).

B. The orthodox position of resurrection as opposed to the immortal soul

Christ's crucifixion and resurrection was necessary as a means to bring about our own resurrection in the future. Christ's death and resurrection were necessary for the forgiveness of the sins of mankind. Paul tells us that righteousness has been credited to us who believe in Christ and what he did. Christ's death and resurrection go together. Paul speaks of the two as separate to accommodate our understanding. Christ's death as the price to pay for our sins brought forgiveness and reconciliation between us and God, and it was completed by his resurrection, verifying our justification through his obedience to sacrifice himself for our sins (Romans 4:23-25).[138]

Furthermore, there would be no salvation if God did not raise Christ from the dead (Romans 5:10; 10:9; First Corinthians 15:17). The resurrection is a necessary part of Christ's work of salvation. The confession is made from the recognition that "our redemption and satisfaction, by which we are reconciled to God, were accomplished by His death, yet the victory over

138 Calvin, John, *The Epistles of Paul the Apostle to the Romans and to the Thessalonians* in *Calvin's Commentaries* series (London: Oliver and Boyd, 1960), 102.

sin, death, and Satan was procured by His resurrection."[139] By confession from the heart, we are exercising the faith that has been given to us (Romans 12:3) in knowing we have been redeemed by what he accomplished for us in our stead.

One is personally justified (or subjectively experiences justification) by believing in Christ. We are called on to receive or accept the gospel, which is about what Christ in his incarnation has accomplished for all mankind. In his death through the eternal Spirit and his resurrection, he has justified all mankind. The gospel is the announcement of this accomplishment of Christ on our behalf, but it must be received as the truth and believed by us individually to be experienced in this life (Second Corinthians 5:18-20). Salvation is an unconditional gift and is received through faith.

Christ's resurrection is just as much a part of the gospel as is his death. Because of Adam's sin, mankind has come under condemnation and has cut itself off spiritually from God and the only source of life. Mankind must face the penalty of death for its sins, but our Trinitarian God, by Jesus' incarnation and sacrifice through the eternal Spirit, has provided the atonement for our sins. It is then through his resurrection that he has made it possible for mankind to experience life after death --- through a resurrection of our own, done through his power. His resurrection is the sign, to us who believe, that this resurrection will come about when he returns.[140] Paul said the gospel is the good news that Christ died for our sins and was resurrected on the third day (First Corinthians 15:1-5).

Christ's resurrection is necessarily important to us, because if we cannot believe that he was resurrected from the grave, then our faith is in vain. And it is significant, not only to those of us who believe, but to the whole human race (First John 2:2). If he remained in the grave, it would mean that he would have only been a rabbi of Nazareth, just another teacher of religion.

139 Ibid., 227.

140 Edward W. , *Beyond Belief* (Philadelphia, PA: The Westminster Press, 1964), 117.

He would be respected for what he taught, but that would not make him the Savior that Christianity believes him to be. The apostles would have been guilty of being false witnesses of the one who is the keystone of our faith, and Christianity as a whole would collapse without him being the Savior sent by the Father to save the world (John 3:16).[141]

Another important aspect to note is that our deceased loved ones would be lost to death forever. Paul said that those who had died and who were even "in Christ," which means believers, would be lost (First Corinthians 15:18). The Greek word translated "lost" here in the NIV has also been translated as "perished," as in the KJV. Either translation would mean that their loved ones would not be in existence in any sense of the word and would never be brought back to life. Only through Christ's resurrection can the dead, whether believers or not, can be brought back to life (First Corinthians 15:14-19).

Moreover, we would also still be in our sins, because they would not have been forgiven, and this would be because salvation accomplished by Christ was a process of several events. He had to die to pay for our sins; he had to be resurrected from the grave as a vindication of its validity, and to complete what was done for us; he also had to ascend to the Father as our representative to present us figuratively as holy and blameless before the Father. The salvation process has been completed as far as Christ was concerned.

Support for the resurrection also comes from what Christ taught. He said that he was the resurrection and the life. There is no life beyond physical death without the resurrection back to life that only comes through Christ. Those who believe in the immortal soul believe the contrary that life as the soul continues on beyond death. For example, Gordon Keddie says that the believer's life continues on at death. The support that he offers

141 John Greenhalgh and Elizabeth Russell, eds., *If Christ Be Not Risen . . . Essays in Resurrection and Survival* (San Francisco, CA: Collins Liturgical, 1988), 10.

is that the *Shorter Catechism* states this as one of the benefits of Christ's death.[142]

Jesus told Martha that her brother, Lazarus, would rise again. She assumed that he meant at the resurrection on the last day. According to Knauft, Jesus then said in answer to Martha,

> "Those who believe in me, even though they die [in this earthly life], will live [at the resurrection on the last day], and everyone who lives [at the resurrection on the last day] and believes in me will never die [forever]. Do you believe this?" She said to him, "Yes, Lord, I believe."[143]

Jesus was talking about the resurrection. To avoid extinction of the entire human race, there will have to be a resurrection back to life. He was the embodiment of the hope of the resurrection back from the dead to life again in the future. Jesus appears to emphasize the importance of the resurrection by equating himself with the resurrection and life. This life must come through the resurrection. All mankind will die and perish if not for his return and the resurrection.

Jesus also taught we can have new life with the Father now, along with our hope in the resurrection. In John 14:6 Jesus is talking about having a relationship with the Father through him. He is the way to the Father. In verses 9-14 he further explains the perichoretic relationship he has with the Father. Then in verses 20-21 he explains that we too, as believers, can experience this relationship with the Father through our relationship with him.

Through Christ's resurrection he has already made us alive spiritually, a life to be experienced only by those who believe, and he has thereby given us a living hope and an eternal inheritance. We talk about the resurrection being the physical resurrection of the person bodily, but there are scriptures

142 Keddie, 427.

143 Daniel Knauft, *Search for the Immortal Soul* (Nampa, ID: Torchlight Intel, 2006), 118.

that also mention what can be called a spiritual resurrection that is directly related to Christ's resurrection. Paul says that due to God's love for us, he has "made us alive with Christ even when we were dead in transgressions" (Ephesians 2:4-5). The Greek word συνεζωοποίησεν, which is translated as "made us alive with," refers to a new spiritual life that we now have with Christ. This is evident by taking into consideration the previous sentence, which says, "we were by nature objects of wrath," and now have been made alive (Ephesians 2:3-4).[144] We were spiritually dead (v. 1) but now are spiritually alive. The meaning is that we have been figuratively raised from a death.

Paul also told us what he taught was his hope. Paul was a Pharisee and had studied as a Pharisee and said that he had the same hope they had. Before the Sanhedrin, as recorded in Acts 23:6-8, he aligned himself with the Pharisaic faction. The Sadducees were turned off by this because they did not believe a resurrection was possible. This caused a dispute between the two groups. But Paul claimed that the reason he was on trial was because of his hope in the future resurrection of the dead.[145] His hope was not in some immortal soul idea that he might live on even when he died, but rather in the idea that Christ would return and resurrect the dead, including him. This was where Paul was in his thinking and belief, and yet people today twist his words in some passages to give the impression that he believed in the immortal soul.

Paul again talks about the resurrection from the dead in Acts 26:6-8. "Two of the most basic future hopes of most Jews were the resurrection of

---

144 Charles J. Ellicott, *Ellicott's Commentaries, Critical and Grammatical, on the Epistles of Saint Paul with Revised Translations* (1978; rpt. Minneapolis, MN: James Family Publishing Co., 1978) I, 47.

145 Gundry, 553.

the bodies of the righteous and the restoration of the twelve tribes at the same time."[146]

A further support comes from theological teaching about our participating figuratively in Christ's acts of salvation. His life was physical in his union with humanity. He lived a perfect life of obedience, free from sin, sanctifying the sinful nature of man. He willingly gave his life physically as an offering to God for our sins, through the shedding of his blood. He was dead and buried physically. Being dead was the price for our sins. Only Jesus of all humans had qualified himself as being innocent of committing any sins, and therefore he did not die for his sins, but for ours.

We know that his resurrection was physical because his body was not left in the grave. He physically rose from the dead to be alive again. He became the firstfruit of mankind that would later be resurrected at his coming for the deliverance of mankind from sin and a fallen world. There is a larger harvest coming beginning at and after the Second Coming as indicated in the Second Thessalonians 2:13, James 1:18 and Revelation 14:4.

His ascension into the heavenly realm was physical, too. He only transcended into the heavenly existence after his physical resurrection. Christ was sent to us by the Father to complete the salvific work for us that we might follow the same pattern that Jesus did in our coming to full salvation. Only by following this same pattern do we identify with Christ in figuratively crucifying ourselves to live a life of obedience to God as Jesus did. All humans will have to be changed or be resurrected from the dead to the heavenly kingdom Christ will establish on earth when he returns, at the end of this world. We will then be what God had planned for us to be through the outworking of his awesome plan of redemption by the Lamb of God for mankind from the beginning of time (Revelation 13:8).

146 Craig S. Keener, *The IVP Bible Background Commentary: New Testament* (Downers Grove, IL: InterVarsity Press, 1993), 399.

C. When and for whom will the resurrection be?

The resurrection is referenced in a number of New Testament scriptures. It will occur on the last day, referring to the last day of this present world, which will end at the coming of Christ to begin the eternal kingdom of God. First Corinthians 15:51-54 tells us that the dead will be raised imperishable, and the mortal will be changed to immortality, at the resurrection. First Thessalonians 4:15-17 also tells us of the dead being resurrected at the coming of Christ.

Moreover, Christ himself tells us when the resurrection that Israel expected will occur. In John 6:38-39 Jesus says that his purpose in coming from heaven was to do the Father's will and to raise the dead "at the last day." This fits also with what was said in John 11:23-24 with respect to what Martha said about Lazarus. She said that she knew Lazarus would be resurrected on the last day, and Jesus added to that, saying, "I am the resurrection and the life."

According to Scripture, there will be a general resurrection that will include all mankind. John 5:28-29 tells us that it will be a resurrection to life and a resurrection to judgment. Those who will be in the resurrection to life are those who have subjectively received Christ as their Savior in this life. They had allowed themselves to be transformed through the sanctification process of living the resurrected life in Christ as his Spirit worked in their lives producing the fruit of the Spirit.

Then we have those who are not subjectively in Christ, who have not accepted Christ as their Savior for a variety of reasons. They may have not heard the gospel in order to be able to accept the message of salvation in Christ, or they may have heard but were not interested in what they heard. Some even may have totally rejected the message as something that they would not be interested in doing.

So we have two groups designated in this general resurrection as to whether they have subjectively experienced the new life in Christ or have not. But regardless of this, all humans are objectively in Christ. It is Christ who has taken the initiative to go through the process of the salvific work to redeem and bring back through the resurrection all who have died in Adam. It is just a matter of their destination at this resurrection that depends on whether they have or have not accepted Christ as their Savior as to whether they will then enter the eternal kingdom or will be separated from those in the kingdom. The converted ones who had subjectively experienced the eternal life that comes from Christ looked forward to the last day, when Christ returns and they would enter into a fuller presence with him in the eternal kingdom.

The others have not experienced that close relationship with the Father in Christ through the Spirit and will be raised to judgment before Christ, who will be their judge. Even though he has been involved in their lives from his standpoint and is, objectively, their Savior in that he has redeemed them, he will not recuse himself from this judgment. He does have a vested interest in them and truly wants them also to repent and come to recognize the Triune God's love for them and to accept it so they also can become a part of the everlasting kingdom. When God in Christ has put all things under Christ, including these who have previously resisted, then it is said that "God may be all in all" (First Corinthians 15:28).

CHAPTER 17: PASTORAL THEOLOGY AND APPLICATION

A. Usual ministry in local churches

1. Serving members

Being pastors of a local congregation, they have to serve their members in a number of ways. They should provide personal counseling and pray with members who have issues to resolve. They are called on to visit the sick, anointing and praying for their healing and affirming to them of the prayerful support of the local church on its behalf.

Pastors offer their services to help members deal with death and the funeral, or memorial services, of friends and loved ones by comforting them in their grief with scriptural promises of the resurrection at Christ's return and our glorious reunion with all of our departed loved ones at that time.

Pastors also should remind members how they can take comfort in that they know Jesus as their Lord and Savior, and they are not going through this situation alone. This is because they have a relationship with Jesus, and he is going through this experience with them. Pastors may at this time have an opportunity to point others present to Jesus as Savior and Lord, and explain how they can have a close relationship with the Father through Jesus in the Spirit.

2. Preaching and teaching

Being pastors, they are responsible for preaching and teaching the congregation, and are to preach the gospel of the good news of God's intervention in the affairs of mankind through the incarnation, death, burial, resurrection, and ascension of Jesus Christ, who through his salvific work healed the breach that was caused by the sin of Adam. The gospel is the announcement of the good news that Jesus' "one act of righteousness was justification that brings life for all men. For just as through the disobedience of the one man the many were made sinners, so also through the obedience of the one man the many will be made righteous" (Romans 5:18-19). The gospel is about entering into a spiritual relationship with the Father by our union in Jesus through the Spirit.

Along with the gospel, they should instruct their members about biblical principles of how to live the abundant life that comes through believing in Christ, and how these principles should be applied in their lives today on a daily basis.

Their Bible studies should be designed to help members understand the Scriptures in the light of the Trinitarian view of God the Father, Son, and Holy Spirit and their inclusion into the relationship with the Father in Jesus through the Spirit. Pastors must try to pass on an interest in the Scriptures, and to challenge their members to study on their own to grow in spiritual maturity as they allow God's Spirit to produce the fruit of the Spirit in their lives (Galatians 5:22-26).

In their Bible studies pastors must try to make everyone feel free to ask any questions as they explain biblical topics. Pastors like discussions of the topic they are teaching. They want to discuss how the biblical principles they see in the texts that they are teaching from can be applied in the lives of those who are attending.

As pastors, they must be approachable by the members. They want them to feel free to come to them with questions and with their personal problems of a spiritual nature. Pastors should be able to take time specifically with them and discuss and pray about their problems.

B. Pastor's Ministry with regard to the immortal soul in the local church

The immortal soul is accepted in most churches because most of the members already believed this idea when they came to the church and probably have believed it from childhood. Ministers in other churches that teach the immortal soul concept encourage their members to witness to others about the gospel of Christ, which becomes the good news of going to heaven instead of hell when you die by believing now in Christ as one's Savior. They are often taught to ask, "If you were to die tonight, do you know that you would go to heaven? If not, then you must give your life to Christ now and be sure that if you die tonight you will be with Jesus in heaven and not end up in hell by rejecting him." Some members may have this background when they come to our church.

Pastors in our churches have a responsibility to correct this where they can and in an appropriate way. They can only deal with this problem on a local level. They can see that their members understand the orthodox teaching of the resurrection, and its importance as a core belief of Christianity. Some members may have a hard time with this, because it has been ingrained in them for years, but a pastor should not compromise with the truth in an effort to let them remain in their comfort zone. This is done as pastors teach the true hope of mankind in their local church through sermons and Bible studies.

1. Through sermons

Sermons must cover these issues from time to time so the congregation is knowledgeable about the importance of the hope of the resurrection of mankind. Sermons must show God's love and desire for the restoration of all mankind, and Jesus and the Father in the Spirit have the same mind of love toward all mankind. Sermons should relate that God was in Christ reconciling all mankind (Second Corinthians 5:18-19) in the eternal Spirit (Hebrews 9:14). All members should know this, and it is good for any visitors to hear this proclaimed. Any who do not know Christ as their Savior should be made aware that they need to believe and receive this objective truth. By accepting this truth, one repents toward God and trusts in Christ as his Savior, being personally reconciled and now knowing that his sins have been forgiven.

In addition to preaching the gospel, it should be made plain that the Bible is talking about the whole man, and not about the spiritual healing of an immortal soul that can at death separate from the physical body and be with the Lord immediately. The Bible is telling us, because of Adam's sin as the representative of mankind, mortality was passed down to all mankind. We all are in the process of dying and will die physically unless the Lord returns prior to our death, but Christ came to redeem us from the consequence of sin, which is death (Romans 6:23). That consequence of mortality will be removed at the resurrection. Christ died, assuming the consequence of Adam's sin as the new representative of mankind, for all of us. Through his death and resurrection for the sake of all, all mankind will be resurrected at his coming (John 5:28-29). God created mankind (male and female) and man became a living soul (being or person). There is nothing indicating that man has a soul or that he is a soul inhabiting a physical body. The soul is the animated person resulting from the combination of the man who was made of the soil of the earth plus the addition of the spirit God breathed into him. One dies when the spirit in man returns back to God who gave it (James 2:26). The body is buried and the soul is no longer. These things must be brought out in sermons and Bible studies from time to time for the church's edification.

2. Through Bible studies

Death according to the Bible is the enemy, but it is temporary. Death was conquered on the cross by Jesus' sacrifice and subsequent physical resurrection to life immortal as a human being. This gives us hope of the resurrection to come as a result of Christ's resurrection, in which he became the firstfruit (The Greek is singular) of the rest of mankind to follow at his return. It can be shown that this was Paul's hope by reviewing portions of first Corinthians 15, where he describes the resurrection of mankind. Paul also said specifically that the resurrection was his hope for life after this life (Acts 23:6). He believed as is recorded in Acts 24:15, "that there will be a resurrection of both the righteous and the wicked." Furthermore, in Acts 26:6-8 he blames his arrest and trial before Agrippa on his hope in the resurrection. He questioned, "Why should any of you consider it incredible that God raises the dead?" He has said all of this about the resurrection to come, but not a word about any immortal soul or a hope to pass into some other realm at death to be with the Lord Jesus.

What he said in First Corinthians 15:17-18 should seal the matter about whether he believed in an immortal soul that could survive the physical death of the body. He said, "If Christ has not been raised, your faith is futile; you are still in your sins. Then those also who have fallen asleep in Christ are lost [or perished]." This says that there is no immortal soul that could bring about their salvation and immediate presence with the Lord. The resurrection by Christ at his coming is necessary. Paul tells us in First Corinthians 15:53-54 that life after death will come about only by the resurrection to immortality.

C. Ministry regarding the immortal soul outside the local church

Pastors must realize that for those Christians outside of our local fellowship, they are going to have to understand that many believe in the idea that their deceased loved ones are in heaven, which may seem more comforting than thinking of them as unconscious until the resurrection. As pastors, however, you are not going to be in a position to change anyone's mind without an opportunity to sit down with them in a Bible study, and with them being willing to take an honest look at the subject from a biblical point of view. One way of reaching people outside of the church is by recommending books in bookstores that we know explain the Biblical understanding about death and the importance of how the resurrection is God's plan to save mankind from perishing.

We also should remember that the salvation of a Christian is not based on how accurate his doctrine is. It is based on Jesus, who is our mediator and redeemer, and who has already provided for the salvation we can experience through believing in him, knowing that we probably will not understand all doctrinal material perfectly. Of course, all Christians should try to learn from Scripture, under the guidance of God's Spirit, the best they can to understand its teachings.

For Pastors, who are called on to preach at funerals, it is tempting to offer a corrective sermon. They have to realize that the purpose of the sermon at a funeral is to give comfort to relatives and friends of the deceased. This is not the time and place for a corrective sermon. As said above, the place to correct this view is in one's own church through sermons and Bible studies, but not among strangers who have come to show their respect through this service given in honor of their loved one. What needs to be foremost in this sermon is God's love for man in that he gave his only Son, Jesus Christ, to die for us, providing the remission of our sins. It is a time to express how it is only through Jesus that this terrible enemy called death will be removed, once and for all. In the meantime we can be assured that the deceased loved one is in God's hands. Our relationship with God is secure in Christ, and death does not separate us from God. Colossians 3:2-4 says, "Set your minds on things above, not on earthly things. For you died, and your life is now hidden with Christ in God. When Christ, who is your life, appears, then you also will appear with him in glory." It should be comforting to know that our loved one's next thoughts will be at the appearance of their Lord and Savior, Jesus Christ.

D. Negative results from ministries teaching the immortal soul

The Bible speaks of death as an enemy. First Corinthians 15:26 says, "The last enemy to be destroyed is death." It is Christ who destroys death. The immortal soul concept teaches that though a person dies, he only dies physically, but he, being the soul and real person, continues on in a disembodied state. It denies the tragedy of death and gives a false comfort to the living that the dead are still alive in another realm of existence.

This immortal soul teaching also weakens the salvific work of Christ. Christ came to redeem us from sin and death, but why did he need to sacrifice himself for us and be resurrected to bring about the resurrection in the future if we have inherently within us the power to continue to live on past our bodily death? It brings the question to mind: Is it really important to have a resurrected body later, when we would already be enjoying life as a soul free of the body with its many limitations? If we are really dead, and there is no immortal soul inherent within us, then it was necessary, as the Bible teaches, that Christ died and rose to give us life again with a new glorious body without the limitations of the flesh-and-blood body we have now. It is only through Christ that we will be released from the bonds of death to live again, and forever be in this everlasting kingdom. To teach otherwise is to deny the teaching of salvation in the Bible.

Related to the salvation issue above, is the fact that when the immortal soul is taught, it reduces one's hope for and expectation of the second coming of Christ. The Bible teaches that the resurrection is to occur at the return of Christ. We are told in Scripture to look forward to that day. It will not matter to us whether we are alive or dead, because either we will be raised from the dead, or changed if we are still alive at that time. For believers, this is the day we enter into our glorious inheritance planned in God's mind before the beginning of the creation of mankind and our universe.

In teaching the immortal soul, there is less regard for the physical world, and for taking good care of our physical world and the pressing need for God's plan to restore nature and the image of God in mankind. God created a beautiful earth for mankind and commanded Adam and Eve to maintain it. We have the responsibility to take good care of his creation. Man should be responsible stewards of this God-given planet, and do what we can to protect it from abuse by others until God brings about the restoration of his creation when Christ returns.

Paul says in Romans 8:19-21,

> The creation waits in eager expectation for the sons of God to be revealed. For the creation was subjected to frustration, not by its own choice, but by the will of the one who subjected it, in hope that the creation itself will be liberated from its bondage to decay and brought into the glorious freedom of the children of God.

E. CONCLUSION

Believers should have the same eager expectation that Paul wrote about, for the restoration of God's creation. The immortal soul doctrine keeps people thinking about their individual salvation out of this fallen world through each one's death, where believers should be looking corporately toward that great day of resurrection when Christ returns, transforming us and this fallen world into the glorious world of tomorrow.

JOHN HUFFMAN

CONCLUSION DRAWN FROM THIS BOOK AS A WHOLE

Our first task was to survey the literature regarding the immortal soul and various beliefs related to it. We found a wide range of beliefs and commented on a number of them, showing where we disagree.

We also showed how the immortal soul is problematic in following biblical teaching about death and the resurrection. It overshadows the doctrine of the resurrection spoken of by Paul as the hope of the believer. We should be looking forward to Christ's Coming when we will be either changed or resurrected to immortality and to a life with Christ. Instead, the immortal soul weakens the believer's expectation of the second coming of Christ, which brings about the resurrection to life in the age to come.

We looked into the historical and literary background of Paul's First Epistle to the Corinthians in preparation for an exegesis of chapter fifteen, where Paul deals with the resurrection, which is basic to our understanding of what happens when Christ returns. We discussed the controversy of whether all, or just believers, will be resurrected. Paul's argument was that all had to be resurrected to counteract the consequences of death that came to all men. If all are not to be raised, then his argument is not complete, and Christ will not counteract and undo what was caused by Adam. We also commented on the phrase "in Christ," which is often taken to mean a reference to believers. We showed how this was, in First Corinthians 15:22, an adverbial phrase that indicated how the resurrection would be accomplished, that Christ was the agent to counteract the consequences brought about through Adam. In the same way, "in Adam" showed what resulted from his sin, not that we had a relationship with him. In First Corinthians 15:22 and 24, we suggested the possibility that those resurrected to judgment, yet spiritually dead, could subsequently "be made alive" (converted and made righteous) after coming to repentance, trusting in Christ, receiving his mercy and the salvation he had already accomplished for them. This then could also mean that the unconverted, who were resurrected spiritually dead, would no longer be spiritually dead, and then it could be said that there is no more death in any sense of the word. This would come under the accomplishments by Christ before turning his kingdom over to the Father, so that God may then be all in all.

In our historical analysis, we showed the origin of the immortal soul. We brought out how there was a period wherein a number of religions developed and how this immortal soul belief entered into Judaism, and then early Christianity. We commented on the meaning of the Hebrew and Greek words translated into the English word "soul," and whether there were scriptures that indicated consciousness or non-consciousness during the intermediate state. We discussed "eternal life" and that the term did not mean immortality. It refers to the spiritual life for this age (the church age) that believers are to live now in Christ as they desire to do in the age to come when Christ returns. Immortality is to be received at the resurrection only.

Later we questioned the texts some say describe the separation of the soul from the body, which is the usual definition given for death by those who believe in the immortal soul. We discussed along with them the idea of eternal torment that often goes with their belief that the soul never dies, but lives on in either heavenly bliss or eternal torment --- in hades at first and finally in Gehenna, after being reunited with a body that will never be consumed, in what they believe to be the everlasting fire.

We supported the orthodox position of Scripture teaching the resurrection. In Adam we all die, but Christ will overturn this tragic consequence by resurrecting the same "all" who die.

Finally, we explained the pastoral theology of serving, preaching, and teaching members in the local church, equipping them to grow spiritually and share the gospel with those with whom they come in contact. With regard to the immortal soul, we seek to teach our members what the Scriptures say, but are careful in dealing with those outside of our local church when it comes to the issue of the immortal soul. We have to show Christian love, understanding that many have grown up with an embedded theology of believing in the immortal soul. The gospel is what is paramount that we share with those outside of our local church, not correction regarding the immortal soul.

Death is our enemy, yet it is denied by believing in the immortal soul. We should be looking with great expectation to the return of Christ, who will be coming to bring about the restoration of humanity to the ideal God had in mind when he created us. God knew man would fail the test of obedience, but he incorporated in his predetermined plan for mankind's destiny that the Son of God would be incarnated to accomplish the righteousness required of man and give himself for our redemption so we could be resurrected as the new humanity in Christ free from our fallen nature.

BIBLIOGRAPHY

Bailey, James L. and Lyle D. Vander Broek. *Literary Forms in the New Testament: A Handbook.* Louisville, KY: Westminster/John Knox Press, 1992.

Bauman, Edward W. *Beyond Belief.* Philadelphia, PA: The Westminster Press, 1964.

Beecher, Edward. *History of Opinions on the Scriptural Doctrine of Retribution.* New York: D. Appleton and Company, 1878.

Beet, Joseph Agar. *The Immortality of the Soul: A Protest.* 2nd ed. London: Hodder and Stoughton, 1901.

Bell, Rob. *Love Wins.* New York: Harper One, 2001.

Bratcher, Robert G. and Eugene A. Nida. *A Translator's Handbook on the Gospel of Mark.* London: United bible Societies, 1961.

Bullinger, E. W. *A Critical Lexicon and Concordance of the English and Greek New Testament.* London: Longmans, Green and Co., 1895.

Calvin, John. *The Epistles of Paul the Apostle to the Romans and to the Thessalonians.* Trans. Ross Mackenzie. Eds. David W. Torrance and Thomas F. Torrance. In *Calvin's Commentaries* series. London: Oliver and Boyd, 1960.

Carson, D.A., R.T. France, J.A. Motyer, and G.J. Wenham. Consulting eds. *New Bible Commentary.* Rev. 4th ed. Downers Grove, IL: IVP Academic, 2010.

D'Souza, Dinesh. *Life After Death: The Evidence.* Washington, D.C.: Regnery Publishing, Inc., 2009.

Ellicott, Charles J. *Ellicott's Commentaries, Critical and Grammatical, on the Epistles of Saint Paul with Revised Translations.* Vol. I. 2 vols. 1978; rpt. Minneapolis, MN: James Family Publishing Co., 1978.

Elwell, Walter A. Gen. ed. *Baker Encyclopedia of the Bible.* "Gehenna," anon. Vol. I. 2 vols. Grand Rapids, MI: Baker Book House, 1988.

———. *Baker Encyclopedia of the Bible.* "Soul," anon. Vol. II. 2 vols. Grand Rapids, MI: Baker Book House, 1988.

Ferguson, Everett. *Backgrounds of Early Christianity.* Grand Rapids, MI: William B. Eerdmans Publishing Company, 1987.

Furnish, Victor Paul. *The Theology of the First Letter to the Corinthians.* New York: Cambridge University Press, 1999.

Gill, John. *An Exposition of the Books of the Prophets of the Old Testament.* Vol. I. 2 vols. In the *Exposition of the Old Testament.* Vol. V. 6 vols. In the *Exposition of the Old and New Testaments* Series. Vol. V. 9 vols. 1989; rpt. Paris, AR: The Baptist Standard Bearer, Inc. 1810.

Gorman, Michael J. *Reading Paul.* Colorado Springs, CO: Paternoster, 2008.

Green, Jay P. Gen. ed. and trans. *The Interlinear Greek-English New Testament: With Strong's Concordance Numbers Above Each Word.* 2nd and rev. ed. Vol. IV. 4 vols. Peabody, MA: Hendrickson Publishers, 1985.

Green, Joel B. "Soul." In *The New Interpreter's Dictionary of the Bible,* ed. Katharine Doob Sakenfeld. Vol. 5 of 5. Nashville, TN: Abingdon Press, 2009.

Greenhalgh, John and Elizabeth Russell, eds. *If Christ Be Not Risen . . . Essays in Resurrection and Survival.* San Francisco, CA: Collins Liturgical, 1988.

Grudem, Wayne. *Systematic Theology: An Introduction to Biblical Doctrine.* Grand Rapids, MI: Zondervan, 1994.

Gundry, Robert H. *Commentary on the New Testament: Verse-by-Verse Explanations with a Literal Translation.* Peabody, Massachusetts: Hendrickson Publishers, 2010.

Guthrie, D. and J. A. Motyer, eds. *The Eerdmans Bible Commentary.* 3rd. ed. Grand Rapids, MI: Wm. B. Eerdmans Publishing Co., 1970.

Hodge, A.A. *The Westminster Confession: A Commentary.* 2002; rpt. Carlisle, PA: The Banner of Truth Trust, 1869.

Holladay, Carl. *The First Letter of Paul to the Corinthians.* Austin, TX: Sweet Publishing Company, 1979.

Jersak, Bradley. *Her Gates Will Never Be Shut: Hell, Hope, and the New Jerusalem.* Eugene, OR: Wipf and Stock, 2009.

Josephus, Flavius. *Josephus: Complete Works.* Trans. William Whiston. Grand Rapids, MI: Kregel Publications, 1960.

Keddie, Gordon J. *A Study Commentary on John.* Vol. I. 2 vols. Auburn, MA: Evangelical Press, 2001.

Keener, Craig S. *The IVP Bible Background Commentary: New Testament.*

Downers Grove, IL: InterVarsity Press, 1993.

Kling, Christian Freidrich. *The First Epistle of Paul to the Corinthians.* Trans. Daniel W. Poor. Vol. VI. of *The New Testament: Containing the Two Epistles of Paul to the Corinthians.* In *The Commentary of the Holy Scriptures: Critical Doctrinal and Homiletical* series. Lange, John Peter. Trans. and ed. Philip Schaff. Vol. X. 12 vols. Grand Rapids, MI: Zondervan Publishing House, 1960.

Knauft, Daniel. *Search for the Immortal Soul.* Nampa, ID: Torchlight Intel, 2006.

Lutzer, Erwin W. *One Minute After You Die.* Chicago: Moody Publishers, 1997.

MacDonald, William. *Believer's Bible Commentary.* Ed. Art Farstad. Nashville: Thomas Nelson Publishers, 1995.

Mills, Liston O., ed. *Perspectives on Death.* New York: Abingdon Press, 1969.

Morris, Leon. *The First Epistle of Paul to the Corinthians: An Introduction and Commentary.* In *The Tyndale New Testament Commentaries* series. Rev. ed. 1990; rpt. Grand Rapids, MI: William B. Eerdmans Publishing Company, 1985.

Morrison, Michael. *Sabbath, Circumcision, and Tithing: Which Old Testament Laws Apply toChristians?* Bloomington, IN: iUniverse, Inc., 2002.

Mounce, William D. *The Analytical Lexicon to the Greek New Testament.* Grand Rapids, MI: Zondervan Publishing House, 1993.

Perkins, Pheme. *First Corinthians.* In *Commentaries on the New Testament* series. Grand Rapids, MI: Baker Academic, 2012.

Plato. *The Apology, Phaedo and Crito of Plato.* Trans. Benjamin Jowett in *The Harvard Classics*, ed. Charles W. Eliot. New York: P.F. Collier and Son Corporation, 1937.

Robertson, Archibald and Alfred Plummer. *A Critical and Exegetical Commentary on the First Epistle of St. Paul to the Corinthians.* Vol. XXXXVI. Vols. 66. In *The International Critical Commentary on the Holy Scriptures of the Old and New Testaments* series. Edinburgh: T. & T. Clark, 1911.

Sabiers, Karl G. *Where Are the Dead?: The Bible Answer.* Los Angeles, CA: Robertson Publishing Company, 1940.

Schultz, Carl. "Soul." In *Evangelical Dictionary of Biblical Theology.* Ed. Walter A. Elwell. Grand Rapids, MI: Baker Books, 1996.

Schwartz, Hans. *Beyond the Gates of Death: A Biblical Examination of Evidence for Life After Death.* Minneapolis: Augsburg Publishing House, 1981.

Spencer, J.A. *Five Last Things: Death, Intermediate State (Hades), Resurrection, Judgment, Eternity.* 3rd ed. New York: Thomas Whittaker, 1892.

Summers, Ray. *The Life Beyond.* Nashville, TN: Broadman Press, 1959.

Trail, Ronald. *An Exegetical Summary of 1 Corinthians 10-16.* 2nd ed. Dallas, TX: SIL International, 2001.

-------. *An Exegetical Summary of Revelation 1 – 11.* 2nd ed. Vol. XXIII. 24 vols. Dallas, TX: SIL International, 2008.

Vine, W.E., Merrill F. Unger, and William White, Jr. *Vine's Complete Expository Dictionary of Old and New Testament Words*. Nashville, TN: Thomas Nelson Publishers, 1996.

Wright, N.T. *Evil and the Justice of God*. Downers Grove, IL: InterVarsity Press, 2006.

-------. *Paul: in Fresh Perspective*. Minneapolis, MN: Fortress Press, 2009.

-------. *Surprised by Hope: Rethinking Heaven, the Resurrection, and the Mission of the Church*. New York: Harper One, 2008.

www.ingramcontent.com/pod-product-compliance
Lightning Source LLC
Chambersburg PA
CBHW021640120626
46545CB00002B/641